Period Finishes
and Effects

Period Finishes and Effects

JUDITH AND MARTIN MILLER

Photography by James Merrell

RIZZOLI
NEW YORK

PERIOD FINISHES AND EFFECTS
Judith and Martin Miller

First published in the United States of America in 1992 by
Rizzoli International Publications, Inc.
300 Park Avenue South, New York, NY 10010

Library of Congress Cataloging-in-Publication Data

Miller, Judith
    Period finishes and effects / Judith and Martin Miller,
        p,   cm.
    Includes index.
    ISBN 0-8478-1569-2
    1. Finishes and finishing.   I. Miller, Martin,   II. Title.
TT305.M628   1992
698—dc20   92-5471
                                                                CIP

Edited and designed by Mitchell Beazley International Ltd
Michelin House, 81 Fulham Road, London SW3 6RB

Chief Contributor: **John Wainwright**

Paint Demonstrators: **Mark Done, Henryk Terpilowski**

Location photography: **James Merrell**
Step-by-step photography: **Paul Bricknell**

Design Director   **Jacqui Small**
Executive Editor   **Judith More**
Senior Art Editor   **Larraine Lacey**
Editorial Assistant   **Jaspal Bhangra**
Production   **Sarah Schuman**
Indexer   **Hilary Bird**

Typeset in Janson and Gill 55   10/12pt. and 75 bold 9/12pt.
by Litho Link Ltd, Welshpool, Powys, Wales
Origination by Scantrans Pte Ltd, Singapore
Printed in Spain by Cayfosa Industria Grafica S.A.

Right:
**A trompe l'oeil print room, with *faux* stone doors and architrave,
painted by Christopher Boulter in the canteen at Kenwood
House, London, England.**

Contents

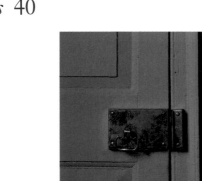

Foreword

*M*y interest in period interiors and furnishings has led, inevitably, to a fascination for period paint effects and surface finishes. The range of finishes used in homes all over the world through the ages is surprisingly extensive. For example, a wall can be decorated with anything from washes of simple paints, made from local ingredients like lime or milk mixed with natural pigments extracted from the earth or from plants, to the most elegant and elaborate hand-printed wallpaper. This book is devised to give an insight into these finishes and effects, their place in history and how they can be utilized in homes today. History should be your servant, not your master. Period style, like any other style, has to be something that you feel happy with.

Although the room schemes shown in this book should not be regarded as the only templates for simulating certain periods, it is important to recognize how a badly chosen, inappropriate effect can alter the feel of a period room. In attempting to create a period style, sensitivity and tact are needed. Flaking milk paint in a grandiose Georgian withdrawing room or a meticulously dragged effect in an Elizabethan beamed kitchen will offend the eye. In order to select a suitable effect for your home, you should always make your choice in relation to its period and also take into account whether it is in a country or an urban setting.

I have always felt that many things combine together to evoke a period feel in a room; the architectural detail, the furniture and the fabrics should not be neglected. But arguably the most subtly important influence on a period mood is the decorative treatment provided by paints, papers, stains and varnishes. One of the beauties of this is that decorative finishes need not be expensive to recreate. Many of the effects can be achieved convincingly at modest expense.

I hope that you will discover, by reading this book, that period-style finishes and effects can be extremely effective in creating a flavour of the past, whether you decide that you prefer recreations that are true to the original – for example, bright gilding – or whether you opt for schemes that are aged and distressed so that they seem to have been carried out in the previous century.

Once you embark on the work in hand, you should find the step-by-step instructions easy to follow and, most of all, great fun to carry out. But before you pick up your paint pot, immerse yourself in this book and let it take you along the path to an inspired choice for your room.   JUDITH MILLER 1992

Right:
As part of the restoration of an 18th-century Rhode Island keeping room, Stephen Mack decorated the simple plank walls with milk paint, now (authentically) flaking due to the presence of moisture in the wood.

Right:
Bare plaster walls convey a sense of age and provide an understated backdrop to the furniture and artefacts in this pastiche of a 19th-century interior – in an authentic recreation the walls would have been decorated.

Introduction

Previous page:
Dragged woodwork, ragged and spattered walls and a trompe l'oeil cornice have been effectively combined in this recreation of a Gothick hallway.

Below:
A 19th-century wallpaper provides the starting point for Jonathan Hudson's judicious use of colour, texture and pattern in his recreation of a Victorian interior.

*T*he variety of decorative finishes and effects that have been used in homes through the ages is enormous. For instance, wall treatments can vary from rough stone, through untreated or painted brick, wood or plaster to luxury finishes such as marble or gold leaf. In the following pages you will be offered a taste of some of the most popular and suitable surface treatments for period homes or period-style decorating schemes.

Following this Introduction, the first chapter of the book looks at the subject of colour. In this section we examine the different ways in which colour has been used over the centuries and in different countries. We also provide useful advice on how to select a suitable colour scheme for your period room.

Many finishes or effects started out in the palaces and mansions of royalty or the aristocracy, and were subsequently copied by the merchant classes. In some cases, we have chosen a grand interior to illustrate one of these finishes – the lavish gilding used to decorate wall mouldings at the Palais de Compiegne in France, for example (*see* the photographs on pp. 120, 121, 122-3) – in order to show an original use of the effect.

Inevitably, intact period schemes are most often preserved in the great historic houses, while those in more modest homes have disappeared. However, we have included plenty of wonderful period recreations carried out in ordinary houses. Often, innovatory work like that at Compiegne was the starting point for a style that was then widely copied, albeit modified by the culture of each region and the constraints of each client's budget. The style favoured by the French court and seen at Compiegne was influential throughout Europe and Scandinavia.

Right:
Gold metallic paint, "knocked back" with a bronze antiquing glaze, mahogany-stained carved woodwork and a modern reproduction (by Watts and Co.) of a mid-19th-century, red and gold patterned wallpaper, provide the sumptuous colouring so evocative of the 19th-century Victorian-Gothic revival.

Other finishes and effects, such as limewash (*see* p.32) and stencilling (*see* p.48) have always had a place in humbler homes as inexpensive methods of decoration. Limewash was one of the first paints and has been used to decorate all manner of homes for thousands of years. It is still used in some country homes to the present day. Its chalky, powdery look is so appealing that many decorators emulate it in the more easily available contemporary paints (*see* pp. 38-9).

Limewash and other traditional formulations for paints can still be found through specialist suppliers if you need to obtain them for authentic restoration work. For safety reasons, many of these traditional paints have to be handled with care and therefore they are generally only used by professionals. If your intention is merely to create a period atmosphere, then carefully chosen modern paints will serve just as well and will be easier and safer to apply.

Some firms produce special paints that emulate the look of the original versions but are formulated with safer modern ingredients for amateurs to use. You can obtain milk paints (*see* pp.44-6) with all the opacity and the authentic rich colour range of the originals but without their harmful lead or lime content, for example.

In the past, paint formulations were not only unsafe, but also unstable. This led to the streaky, uneven effects that are imitated today by dragging and ragging (*see* pp. 56 and 65). These broken colour techniques were originally developed by decorative painters as part of a library of skills needed to produce the illusory *faux* finishes such as marbling (*see* pp.106-113) or stonework (*see* pp.115-9, tortoiseshelling (*see* pp.128-9) and graining (*see* pp.93-105). These finishes have been used for many centuries to replicate expensive, often unobtainable materials. They were commonly employed to simulate panelling on walls or to decorate objects like boxes or picture frames.

Methods of applying paint have changed with time, too. In ancient Egypt the art of fresco – painting into wet plaster – was developed (see p.40). This process was used both to simply tint walls with flat colour and, more elaborately, by artists to produce murals on walls. Painters also worked directly onto dry plaster and wooden surfaces. Only with the development of wallpaper was paint applied onto plaster lined with paper.

Wallpaper (*see* pp.146-153) started to compete with paint during the 18th century, and in the 19th century mass-production of wallpaper gave it the edge over paint as a main wall treatment in many homes. From its earliest days as small hand-painted or printed panels used only in the grandest homes to the machine age when factory-printed rolls hung in the humblest cottage, wallpaper became a decorative finish that was accessible to all levels of society. (Although in far-flung corners of 19th century America and Scandinavia paper was unobtainable and therefore stencilled or hand-painted patterns were used as a substitute.) The advances in printing processes that took place with the Industrial Revolution enabled manufacturers to produce a vast range of wallpapers to suit all purses and tastes.

Technological progress has affected other surface treatments. For example, the formulations for waxes and polishes (*see* p.86) have moved on from simple beeswax polishes to silicon sprays. In this case, advances have not necessarily been to the long-term benefit; beeswax polish may be harder to apply, but it is safer to the health of humans and the environment than a silicon spray. And it is somehow much more satisfying to apply, perhaps because of its attractive smell. It is also much the best treatment for antique furniture because not only does it help to build up a beautiful patina of age, but it can also be easily removed whenever a piece needs refinishing. In contrast, if you allow a silicon polish to get into the grain of a piece of antique wooden furniture you will have caused it lasting detriment.

As well as looking at the history of traditional finishes and effects, and the methods

Below:
Colourwashed, rough-plastered walls provide a strong and simple architectural framework for this Spanish country *finca*.

Below:
Marbled walls and contrasting marbled skirting provide an authentic backdrop to this North American Empire-style study.

Below:
A fine example of Elizabethan bleached carved oak panelling, at Parham House in Sussex, England.

used to produce them, this book examines all the different ways in which you can create an antique look on a new surface, whether it be metal, wooden, painted or plastered. For instance, metal can be treated with patinating fluid (*see* p.130) to give it an antique look. And raw new wood can be aged (*see* pp.80-5) in order to blend in with a period scheme, while bright, fresh paintwork can be distressed (*see* pp.68-79) to give it an impression of age and wear. These antiquing skills involve both distressing an actual material with special tools or chemicals as well as simulating a distressed material in paint.

Such devices are not new to this century – 18th century French painters invented the craquelure technique (*see* p.76) in order to simulate the crazing that appears with age on new paint. And the Victorians blackened their carved oak Elizabethan and Gothic-style furniture with stains to give it the appearance of old wood darkened by smoke, soot and the effects of age.

When planning how you are going to decorate your interior, you should not feel bound to replicate a period scheme using the original materials if they are hard to obtain, expensive or difficult to use. Unless you are dealing with a significant period property, this would be a waste of money and effort. Half the fun of creating a period room is indulging in the theatrical art of illusion.

Whether you feel competent enough to create an elaborate trompe l'oeil (*see* pp. 136-143) or prefer to stick to a simple task such as pasting photocopies of prints onto the wall in the manner of an 18th-century print room (*see* pp.157-61), your degree of success will be dependent on your ability to capture a period mood just as much as on any technical skills you may have.

At the heart of this book are the chapters detailing the history and uses of each technique. Where appropriate, we examine both the orthodox approach to the subject and the simulator's route. Each chapter is also accompanied by easy-to-follow step-by-step instructions, illustrated with colour photographs, showing period-style decorative techniques being carried out on a particular object or surface.

To enable you to carry out these techniques on any surface and in any situation, the chapters on the individual finishes are followed by a comprehensive reference guide to materials, equipment and further techniques. This section gives all the background advice today's decorative painter will need when choosing and using specialist equipment and tools. It also includes detailed instructions on how to prepare surfaces and how to mix paints and glazes.

The book concludes with a Directory of suppliers of paints, papers and other products for those of you who want to try the techniques for yourselves. This listing also includes the details of selected decorative artists and interior decorators for those of you who prefer to commission a professional to recreate an effect for you.

Finally, a word of advice before you embark on your period-style decorating project. The work of creating a scheme should not stop when you put down your brush or close your can of paint. Although the right finish is a very important part of creating a period look, it isn't the only essential ingredient. You shouldn't neglect those finishing touches that will make all the difference to creating a real period atmosphere. Take time to drape your windows with fabrics produced to period patterns, and try to find one or two pieces of antique furniture to set the style. Then light your rooms with candles and position an appropriate ornament where it will catch the eye.

Overleaf:
Tinted with a locally available terracotta-coloured pigment, these colourwashed walls harmonize with a terracotta tiled floor and chestnut shutters to provide an authentic background to a selection of 19th-century Italian country furniture. The rich colour glows against the warm light in this late 18th-century priest's house in Tuscany, Italy.

Below:
Terracotta and deep green create a rich contrast in the stairwell of an 18th-century French townhouse.

Below:
Marbled-panelled walls complement the marble table top and pedestal in this Italian-inspired London apartment.

Below:
An 18th-century French town house decorated by Comoglio in period colours and document wallpaper.

Colour

Since prehistoric times, when man discovered how to use pigments derived from earth and vegetable matter to decorate surfaces, colour has been a key element in interior decoration. Colours were produced from local ingredients and therefore the range was limited by what was available in that region. Artists' Indian yellow, for example, was originally made from earth mixed with cattle urine. Iron oxide, ochre and umber were also common paint colourants. However, as trade and industry developed, decorators gained access to a wider and wider range of colour pigments.

Man's environment has always influenced colour choice. For example, many inhabitants of the 19th-century cities avoided using light colours in their homes because the soot and pollution in the air dirtied them very quickly and therefore they had to redecorate more often. Whereas in the country the colour palette was different. Pollution was not such a problem and fashion less of an influence, but access to products could be, so colours were often based on easily available pigments.

Some country colours were found in many continents; a blue-green colourwash for wooden panelled walls was used throughout Scandinavia, America and in England. Mixed in situ by itinerant painters, the blue-green colour was derived from the earth pigment *terra verde* (green earth), mixed with egg white and buttermilk.

Choosing colours for a period restoration project would be a straightforward task if a chart specifying particular colours for particular periods could be produced. However, although it is possible to identify modish schemes from certain periods, such schemes were not necessarily common, they did not preclude other colour schemes and they did not disappear altogether once their moment had passed. (Indeed, many schemes, such as the white and gilt combination that is most closely associated with the 18th century, have enjoyed numerous high fashion revivals.)

Genuinely new colours are rare and emerge as a result of industrial progress – like the development of chemical pigments in the 1870s – rather than in response to decorator's

demands. And some hues disappear when it is realized that their traditional ingredients are unsafe. Some decorators' colour pigments have turned out to be highly toxic – to the extent of having unexpected influences on the course of history. Napoleon's death has been attributed to the inhalation of arsenic fumes produced by the Emerald Green pigment that was used to colour his bedroom wallpaper.

Today, there are three main sources that will help you to make your choice of an appropriate period colour scheme. This documentary evidence can consist of early treatises on decorating, paintings of the period that show interior settings and artefacts from the period on which the original colour is known to be intact. Perhaps the best source of inspiration can be found in the china cabinet since glazes on porcelain preserve colours in a very true manner. You will find that studying some typical pieces of 17th- or 18th-century Wedgwood, Meissen or Sevres ware could provide you with an authoritative reference for suitable colours and colour combinations. Records relating to the production of colour pigments date back to medieval Europe. During this period of history the secrets of the methods used to make pigments were controlled by colourists, who had their own guild. Would-be colourmen served an apprenticeship in the orthodox methods of mixing and grinding colours for the painter or dyer to use. Medieval buildings, whether constructed for secular or religious purposes, were very colourfully painted, inside and out, with wooden beams picked out in rich hues and with heraldic devices or patterns decorating plaster panels.

Polychromatic colour schemes were popular up until the 17th century. However, by the end of the 17th century white walls decorated with gilded mouldings became the *sine qua non* for state rooms in French palaces and throughout the 18th century this fashion filtered down through society.

However, it was not until about 1750 that light schemes took hold in the English-speaking world, Holland and Germany. During the 18th century these French-influenced pale colours had also reached Scandinavia. In Sweden, Andreas Lindblom described walls that were "pink, mid-blue, apple green, straw yellow, and above all *perl grott* or pearl gray. Gilding is restricted to mouldings and ornament. White is never used, and marbling sparingly. Pleasure and cheerfulness animate this decorative scheme".

During the 18th century brighter colours also became popular, particularly for painting panelling. In 1752, the French writer Blondel

Above and below:

Terracotta and blue paints prepared from local pigments enhance the walls of a villa in Tuscany, Italy.

Below:

A modern paint in a soft green shade is true to the period spirit of this 18th-century wooden panelling.

mentions *jonquille*, *citron*, blue, green and yellow being used as treatments for panelling in smaller rooms. (White continued to be used for the grander salons.) Ceilings were treated in a similar manner to the walls, with moulding details picked out in gold against either a white or a coloured ground.

By the middle of the 18th century in England flat colour was being used as a foil to rich decorative techniques such as graining (*see* pp.93-105), marbling (*see* pp.106-113) and gilding (*see* p.126). While in North America, the Colonial palette combined earth colours like almond, red and brown with very bright blues, greens and yellows. And the later Federal taste included terracottas and deep pinks, along with stone colours and also gray.

By the time of the British architect Robert Adam in the late 18th century, the academic study of the human response to colour had begun. In 1766, one of the earliest publications on the subject, "The Natural History of Colours", by Moses Harris, was dedicated to the British artist Sir Joshua Reynolds, the first President of the Royal Academy. In his treatise, Harris attempted to divide 15 colours into 20 degrees of power that produced over 300 tints.

Awareness of colour principles was growing in France, too. Jacques Christophe le Blon, a painter working at the French court in 1730, noted that red, yellow and blue were primary colours in paints which, if intermixed, produced orange, green, violet and other hues.

Adam made use of these newly discovered principles in order to distinguish one moulded form from another and thus strengthen the impression of three-dimensionality. In addition to employing classical colour combinations like white, blue and cream, recorded as a scheme for a ceiling in the early 1770s, the original colours chosen by Adam for his schemes could be surprisingly bright. He was known to have used sharp pale blues, greens, pinks and cerises.

Although 18th-century colours could be very vivid, with hues like turquoise, pea green and Chinese yellow finding popular favour, the composition of the paints available at this time was quite unstable and therefore the strength of the colours waned very rapidly.

Elaborate schemes of the late 18th- and early 19th-centuries usually involved treating walls and ceilings as a whole. The English designer Sheraton writes: "When the profiles of rooms are of gilt, the ceilings ought likewise to be gilt." He also comments that "The usual method is to gild the ornaments and leave the ground white, pearl colour, light blue, or any other that may be proper to set off the gilding to advantage".

By the 1830s it had become the vogue to tint ceilings because white was considered to make too stark a contrast to coloured walls. In British writer John Loudon's "Villa Companion" of 1838, he describes a breakfast room ceiling that is gray or light green, with the ceiling mouldings or cornice tinted to a slightly darker shade.

In general, walls were decorated in light colours during the first quarter of the 19th century. The exceptions were libraries, dining and drawing rooms, where darker shades were sometimes used. James Arrowsmith writes in about 1830 of English drawing room walls "panelled with watered silk of pearl white, or light tints of pink, or lavender". Of the darker shades, crimson was the most commonly used, particularly in dining rooms where, John Loudon states, "few colours look better than a deep crimson paper in flock". The ceiling and the ceiling mouldings or cornice would be tinted to match the colour of the walls.

In Scandinavia, too, warm pastels such as the old pink colour known as *gammel rosa* were in vogue. This shade had the advantage of looking gray in natural light, but appearing as a rosy shade when viewed under candle or oil light.

By the second half of the 19th century, strong colours were popular once more. It is often assumed that these High Victorian schemes were sombre and muddy in hue, but in fact this is not the case. Surviving evidence of original treatments may lead observers to conclude this because of the effects of pollution, sunlight and time on fugitive dyes. However, when new these colours were rich, possibly dark, but almost always very vivid.

The invention of aniline dyes in the mid 19th century created a fashion for sharp yellows, intense blues and acid greens of a chemical intensity that had not been seen before. Even when earthy reds or deep browns were used, they were brightened with gold or bright yellows. The new colours were first used for textiles, and were then introduced into wallpapers before going on to influence paint tints. Experimentation with these new shades led to some quite lurid, tasteless colour combinations, such as purple and mustard, being used.

Partly as a reaction to this, muted colours were popular among followers of the Arts and Crafts Movement. They even inspired a new description of a colour, "greenery-yallery", for the muted olive green that was so favoured by Aesthetic designers, particularly for wood-

Above and below:

Throughout the Mediterranean you will find rich terracotta and blue. These examples are from Spain and Gran Canary.

Below:

In the hallway of a 19th-century house colour contrast is used to highlight the division of a wall by a dado moulding.

work. Ebonized black wood treatments were also popular. Other favourites for walls were burgundy, old rose and hyacinth blue.

For Aesthetic rooms which were used in the daytime light colours were also used, with schemes based on several shades of white – from ivory to pale gray – being quite common. Similar shades – whites, plus muted greens, lilacs, purples and black were also popular for Art Nouveau schemes. Some of the best examples of colour treatments for this style can be seen in the work of the Glasgow architect Charles Rennie Mackintosh.

The early years of the 20th century saw a return to pale schemes and a growing use of white as cities became cleaner. Writing in 1904, the London decorator Cowtan notes that "we seem to have done everything flatted white or enamelled white paint. The question of whether it was suitable or not with the decoration was entirely lost sight of."

The neo-classical revival that begun in the 1880s and continued in the first quarter of the 20th century brought back white and gold schemes, along with Wedgwood blue, oyster, lilac and stone-gray.

The move away from colour accelerated with the rise of the Modern Movement. One of the most well-known interiors of the decade was the "All-White Room" created in 1929 by the decorator Mrs Syrie Maugham in her house in Chelsea, London, England. And in the United States decorator Elsie de Wolfe was producing similar work. During the 1930s, the fashion for lighter colours spread, and owners of humbler homes began to change their dark walls and fabrics to buffs, beiges, coffee, pastel blue or pink or the ubiquitous eau-de-nil.

However, it would be a mistake to assume that for modernists any colour went so long as it was white. Throughout the early years of the 20th century there was a parallel trend that promoted the use of strong colours. At the *Exposition des Arts Decoratifs*, which was held in Paris in 1925 and launched the Art Deco movement onto the international scene, vividly coloured schemes were on show. These included a yellow and black living room by designer François Jourdain and a purple and black dining room from Paul Poiret's Atelier Martine.

Other startlingly rich colours used in Art Deco schemes included ultramarine, crimson, burnt orange and deep blue. Colour combinations were bold. For example, glossy black walls were combined with either red or silver woodwork or deep blue walls were paired with red woodwork.

In complete contrast to the saturated

colours and sparkling whites of the modern movement, the vogue for combining antique furniture with mellow period-style paint treatments or document papers and fabrics recreated from archive material became a classic decorating trend during the 20th century. Faded beyond recognition by time, surviving examples of 18th and 19th-century rooms have persuaded some 20th-century restorers or copyists to use a completely different set of colours to the actual originals. And so throughout the 20th century neo-classicists have employed soft, muted pastels for their 18th-century style schemes, while from the 1960s onward neo-Victorians decorated their homes with dark, muddy browns, reds and greens.

In the early years of the 20th century Nancy Lancaster and John Fowler undertook painstaking research into original period colour schemes. They chipped paints down to reveal original layers and then mixed up colours to match. Fowler worked with the English National Trust on the restoration of many important houses using this technique.

Because of the high degree of lead used in 18th-century paint it was quite difficult to reproduce the luminosity of the original. Following this ground-breaking approach, several companies were set up which

Above:
The rich red-painted walls of this music room in a restored American Empire-style house were colour-matched to the original early 19th-century finish.

Right:
The woodwork in this room has been decorated with a green milk paint; colour-matched to the original 18th-century paint.

Above:

In addition to paler hues, bright blue, red and yellow were fashionable wall colours throughout much of the 18th century.

Left:

Vivid matte blue-green painted joinery lends a South American ambience to this room in an 18th-century farmhouse in Maine, North America.

specialize in producing period-style paints (*see* the Directory, pages 172 and 174). Some of these firms have even gone to the extent of manufacturing a lead substitute to give historic colours an authentic appearance.

Unlike Nancy Lancaster and John Fowler, you probably won't be able to take paint samples to find the original colour of your room, but you can follow the advice given on p.20 for alternative ways of selecting appropriate colours. Befcre you make your final choice of colour, it is essential to examine the paint under both daylight and artificial light, so that you can see how the effect will look at different times of day. Ideally, you should brush out a swatch of the genuine article, rather than relying on a printed colour card.

You also need to decide whether you want to recreate the original bright colour scheme that would have been chosen a century or more ago, or whether you would prefer a time-worn, faded version. There are numerous ways to age colours; John Fowler antiqued white with a dash of artist's raw umber paint for a mellow tone that was exactly right for the period English country homes he decorated. Whichever approach you choose, you will find instructions for different finishes and advice on paints in the chapters that follow.

Left:
Chocolate-brown walls, subtly dragged and spattered with gold and silver, complement the lustrous patination of mahogany furniture and richly coloured fabrics in the bedroom of a city apartment. The architectural proportions of the room are emphasized by the application of a contrasting pale green paint on the window frames and *faux marbre* skirting boards (baseboards).

Above:
Distressed matte-green paint on the wall panelling and built-in four-poster bed and bookshelves lends this small early Georgian-style bed chamber an appropriately restful air. A vibrant contrast is provided by the red silk canopy above the bed; the red and green heightening each other's chromatic intensity, with potentially stimulating results.

Right:
**The wooden
panelling and
cupboard doors in
this 18th-century
North American
keeping room have
been redecorated
with authentic
Colonial-red milk
paint. (For a list of
suppliers of
traditional milk
paints *see* pages 172-
175).**

Right:
**By decorating the
wooden wall
panelling with
authentic
Williamsburg blue
milk paint, the
owners of this newly
built North
American home
have given it the feel
of an original 18th-
century Chester
County plank
house.**

Top:
The guest bedroom of Richard Jenrette's house on the Hudson River in North America has been redecorated in the original early 19th-century colour scheme of deep mauve and yellow.

Above:
The wall panelling in this 1720s interior has been repainted in the original "white". The overmantel board was painted by Tom Hickman in 1989, from an 18th-century print.

Top:
Matte-blue wall panelling, colour-matched to the original paint, and a stencilled floor provide the perfect setting for Sheraton-style chairs (*c.* 1820) and a Federal D-end dining table.

Above:
Comoglio's restoration of an 18th-century French *salon* includes document fabrics and a colour scheme copied from a *salon* at Jean-Jacque Rousseau's house, *Les Charmettes*, in France.

Top:
Matte-red painted woodwork, waxed floorboards and vegetable-dyed rugs provide an authentic setting for period furniture in an 18th-century house in London, England.

Above:
Jonathan Hudson's recreation of a late 19th-century interior was inspired by Sir Lawrence Alma-Tadema's painting of Linley Sambourne House in Stafford Terrace, London, England.

Top:
Wine-red paint and gilding is contrasted with the pale green wall panelling and helps to define the architectural proportions of an alcove in the Georgian town house shown *left*.

Above:
Note how the chromatic intensity and hue of the matte-blue painted wall panelling, also shown *opposite top right*, "changes" under natural (as *here*) and artificial light (as *opposite*).

Top:
The walls of this Colonial-style Canary Island *salon* have been decorated in soft shades of pink and peach. The blue painted joinery was "aged" by first scrubbing with soap and water and then rubbing in an oil-based glaze tinted with burnt sienna artist's pigment.

Above:
The rough-plastered walls of an inner courtyard in Christopher Gollut's village house in Gran Canary have been colourwashed in a "cool" blue that gently contrasts with the pale wooden joinery, earth-coloured flagstone floor and *faux* stonework doorways.

Left:
The terracotta-coloured walls of this terrace in Southern Spain provide a subtle and harmonious contrast with the surrounding countryside, and lend an "established" look to what is in fact a recently built house.

$\mathscr{L}imewashing$

Below left and right:
The rough-plastered walls of this cob house in North Devon, England, have been limewashed to protect them from decay. Limewash allows moisture in the cob walls to evaporate.

*A*s a protective and decorative finish for plaster, render, masonry and to a lesser extent wood, limewash had been in common use for thousands of years prior to the middle of the 19th century. The earliest examples have been found on primitive dwellings *c.* 8000 BC. Although limewashing declined with the advent of modern building materials and synthetic paints, it remains both aesthetically desirable and an essential protective finish for many buildings constructed of traditional materials.

While consituents have varied slightly, the basic wash is made by slaking lump lime in water to produce lime putty. The putty is then mixed with water and a water-proofing agent such as tallow (an animal fat) to produce a milk-like wash. Applied untinted and in several coats, the wash dries to a "pure" white that changes subtly in appearance depending on light and weather conditions. For example, it can appear as a dazzling luminous white, best associated with the vernacular architecture of the Mediterranean, or take on a darker, matte chalky appearance when wet or under over-cast conditions, such as often prevail in Northern Europe.

As an alternative to the basic whitewash, pigments (usually those locally available) can be added; primarily earth colours and by-products of the mining industry, such as iron-and chrome-oxide, cobalt, copper carbonate and cadmium colours. Enhanced by the lime-wash base, they display a vitality and purity of colour, and a mellowing with age, that is rarely matched by synthetic paints.

Apart from being aesthetically pleasing, the most important characteristic of limewash is that it allows the underlying surface to "breathe". Walls made from traditional materials such as wattle and daub and cob (clay subsoil and chopped straw), and lime renders and plasters, absorb moisture from their surroundings and decay if permanently saturated. Applications of semi-porous limewash minimize absorption, allow evaporation of damp, and thus help to preserve the substrate.

Owing to the caustic nature of slaked lime, limewash also has good disinfectant properties. On half-timbered buildings, wooden panelling and unpainted furniture – an application prevalent in Medieval Europe (and some tropical countries to this day) – limewash was used as a deterrent to woodworm and other insect infestation. Similarly, for reasons of hygiene, there was a tradition of scrubbing down the walls of country kitchens and repainting them with limewash every spring. (For a simulation of this finish using modern paints, see page 38.)

Although most commonly associated with rural architecture, notably farm houses and

Right:
A terracotta-coloured *faux* limewash effect on the walls and ceiling contributes to the cottage-like appearance of Guimond Mounter's early 20th-century house in Devon, England.

Below:
When mixing limewash, always brush out a test swatch to see if you have achieved the desired colour, or need to adjust the quantity of pigment. Note that the colour appears darker when wet (*bottom*) than when dry (*top*), and the more coats applied, the more intense the basic hue becomes.

A *Limewashes*

  A Red-brown
B **B** Marigold
  C Black
  D Terracotta
C **E** Brown umber
  F Light brown
D **G** Yellow brown
  H Red

E A selection of
   traditional earth-
F coloured limewashes,
   all of which will
   mellow with age. On
G internal surfaces at
   least three thin coats
H are required; four or
   five outside.

country cottages, limewash was also used on civic and religious buildings and grander domestic dwellings. The Romans used it on Hadrian's Wall, and the White Tower at the Tower of London has been limewashed since its construction at the end of the 11th century. In Medieval times, walls and the wooden or stone mullions of windows were lime-washed in flat white or earth colours, often as a background for geometric patterns, flower motifs and murals. Similarly, unpanelled walls in many Tudor and Elizabethan houses were limewashed and augmented with stencils or wall-hangings.

Throughout Europe during the 17th, 18th and early 19th centuries, limewash remained in common use on the rough plasterwork walls of country cottages, as well as in the less important rooms of larger houses. In America – where the vernacular architecture of Pueblo and Spanish New Mexican cultures had long been decorated with limewash – 18th-century Colonial style featured smooth or rough plastered walls, often part-panelled and lime-washed in white or strong, matte earthy colours. And in Scandinavia, limewash was the predominant external finish on civic and domestic architecture (until the 1950s), in colours ranging from cream ochre through salmon pink and russet to tawny orange.

For colourwashing internal walls, limewash was gradually supplanted by distemper (*see* page 168). Made from whiting, water, animal glue and powder pigment, distemper was easier to mix and apply and, more importantly, less hazardous to health – the slaking of lime in water to make lime putty produced toxic fumes harmful to the lungs of the workers who mixed it on site.

With the introduction of new building materials in the 19th century, limewashing also became either unnecessary or unsuitable as an exterior finish. A damp course and the use of hard cement renders, modern bricks and other impervious materials, meant that walls no longer needed to "breathe". Wallpapers could be safely used inside, while non-porous oil-based paints and (by the 1950s) latex (vinyl) emulsions offered protection both inside and outside.

However, for buildings constructed of traditional materials, limewash has remained an essential, authentic and desirable finish. Instructions on its suitability for different surfaces and how to safely prepare and apply it are given on page 168. A list of suppliers along with the addresses of organizations offering helpful advice on the subject can be found in the Directory on pages 172-5 at the back of the book.

Overleaf:
An off-white limewash has been used on the rough-plastered bedroom walls of a Tuscan house, near Montalchino in Italy, which was formerly the residence of the local priest. The finish provides an appropriately understated and restful backdrop to the collection of paintings and the simple yet elegant fixtures and country furniture on display in the bedroom.

Above, below and right:
Pale pastel and traditional earth-coloured *faux* limewash effects have been used on the walls throughout this house in Devon, England. The finish is a natural complement to the wood parquet flooring, plain boards and many fine examples of provincial period furniture displayed in antique dealer Guimond Mounter's West Country home.

Right: Traditionally used over bare plaster, limewash can also be applied to lining paper.

The technique shown here for simulating a weathered limewash (or distemper) finish using modern synthetic paints should not be used on cob walls. The composition of these walls is such that they must be decorated only with traditional paints, which allow them to "breathe". Modern paints don't do this, and consequently will eventually cause structural damage.

If you wish to experiment with alternative colour combinations to the one shown here, refer to the traditional limewash colour swatches shown on page 34.

Limewashing effect

4 Finally, if the walls are likely to be subject to particularly heavy wear and tear they can be given a protective coat of clear matte water-based varnish.

Paints and Glazes

A Off-white latex (emulsion) paint.

B 3 parts light brown eggshell paint, 1 part mineral spirits (white spirit).

C Pale beige latex (matte emulsion) paint.

A
B
C

1 Begin by applying one or two coats of paint A to the previously prepared walls. Allow each coat to dry for roughly four hours.

Next, dip the bristle tips of a large standard decorator's brush into paint B and, having brushed off most of the paint onto a piece of paper, dry-brush what's left in all directions over the walls. Keep repeating this procedure until you have built up a mottled, cloudy expanse of colour. Then leave to dry overnight.

1

2 Repeat dry brushing using pale beige paint C. However, this time leave more paint on the bristles in order to produce a smoother, less brushy coat which allows very little of the underlying colour to show through. Then again leave the surface to dry for approximately four hours.

2

3 Dampen a kitchen scourer with water and scrub down the walls. This will soften up the top coat, cutting it back in places to reveal patches of the underlying colour, as well as spreading a thin, translucent veil of the top colour over the entire surface. Allow to dry for up to eight hours.

3

Plaster finishes

Historically, decorative plaster finishes can be divided into two main categories. The first, known as fresco (from the Italian for fresh), basically involves mixing pigments with water and applying them to a plaster surface that is still wet. The second, known as fresco *secco* (from the Italian for dry), involves decorating the plaster with pigments mixed with water after it has dried. Examples of the first category – "pure" fresco – are quite rare, owing to the fact that many pigments undergo undesirable chemical changes when applied to wet plaster, with the result that the painter or artist finds it difficult to guarantee the colour of his or her work. Consequently, many frescoes are

in fact created using a combination of the wet and dry methods: the "stable" pigments being applied first to the wet plaster and the "unstable" pigments, having been mixed with a binding or fixing agent, applied second once the plaster has dried.

As far as durability is concerned, the "pure" fresco technique has both advantages and disadvantages. On the one hand, the fact that as the plaster dries a process of carbonation occurs which binds the pigments into a reflective, crystalline surface, means that the finish is relatively hard-wearing and the pigments are less prone to rubbing off, flaking and crazing and, to some extent, fading under direct sunlight,

than they would be if applied using the fresco *secco* technique. On the other hand, "pure" fresco is particularly vulnerable to moisture. This explains why the "pure" fresco technique is largely confined to the warmer, drier climes of Southern Europe, while the fresco *secco* method is the preferred method in Scandinavia and Northern Europe, where the prevailing climate is colder, wetter and therefore less humid.

Plaster walls were being frescoed as early as the 3rd century BC, when Egyptian painters used powdered pigment dispersed in gum to colour flat stucco walls on the inside of tombs. The frescoes were almost invariably representations of significant events from the occupant's life, and were intended to help or guarantee his or her continued journey in the afterlife. As such, the frescoes had a religious significance, and thus both their style and their subject matter were strictly controlled by the dictates of the priests, rather than being left up to the imagination of the painter or artist.

Perspective, which had yet to be discovered, was not used in these early examples of fresco painting. Instead, the lower register of the wall served as the foreground of the scene, while the higher register located the background. This is a simple but effective device which makes this form of decorative painting much easier to reproduce than the trompe l'oeil techniques developed (*see* pages 136-143) in later centuries.

The use of fresco as a means of decoration eventually spread from tombs to the walls of secular dwellings. In Ancient Greece, for example, plaster walls were often painted in tempera mixed with a binding medium, red being the most popular colour.

Many early fresco paintings, executed by Greek artists for Roman clients, have been preserved at Pompeii, the Roman town that was buried by the eruption of the volcano Vesuvius in AD 78. Rich, deep colours were used, particularly vermillion. This pigment was mixed with hot wax before being applied to the wall because the wax further enriched the colours and gave the surface a particularly lustrous sheen.

Artists and painters of the time employed a variety of ingenious techniques to achieve high-quality results, including the use of fat to neutralize the acidity of the lime content of the plaster, which would have otherwise eventually caused a chemical breakdown in the pigments that were applied on top. Also, when mixing and adjusting the strength of their paints and washes they became adept at assessing the degree to which the wet colours

would become lighter as they gradually dried out on the wall.

Painting directly onto plaster, whether wet or dry, continued to be used throughout the Medieval period. Walls were often covered in tempera or plaster, then washed with colour using a mixture of pigment, powdered chalk or whiting and water. A grid of simple red lines intended to represent masonry blocks was sometimes added (an early form of trompe l'oeil stoneblocking, *see* page 115) and heraldic devices and designs copied from illuminated manuscripts were also used to decorate the plaster. Such embellishments were either added freehand, or by the use of stencils – the latter method being ideal for anyone of limited artistic abilities who wishes to recreate this period effect today.

During the Renaissance, sections of walls not covered by paintings, tapestries or other hangings would often be decorated with

Above:
The walls of a room in a late 18th-century priest's house near Montalchino in Tuscany, Italy, have been decorated with a traditional blue colourwash tinted with locally available sienna powder pigments.

Left:
The fresco-embellished, plastered walls of this Italian house display signs of weathering and the ravages of pollution – an effect that can be simulated with the use of a hammer, bolster and sandpaper.

fresco panels or friezes. Indeed, Italian fresco painting continued to play a significant role in decorative schemes for interiors up until the Rococo period. However, as the production of, and demand for, first fabrics and later papers to cover and decorate walls increased, painting directly onto plaster began to fade from fashion.

From the 18th century onward, even plain painted walls were commonly lined with paper prior to painting. There was one exception to this: entrance halls, which would be of painted plaster and sometimes varnished to produce a lustrous, high-sheen finish if the client demanded it. However, fresco work did not die out altogether, although it chiefly survived as a device for creating an "antique" look. For example, in 1799 Venanzio Maruglia designed fresco murals for the King's Bedroom at the Palazzina Cinese, in Palermo, Sicily. He even artificially "aged" his work by deliberately adding damp marks and stains to the finish!

Similarly, in Regency England there was a vogue for decorative schemes that included designs inspired by surviving wall paintings at Pompeii, Italy. Archaeologists had first excavated the buried Roman town in the mid-18th century, and the wall decorations were described in John Goldicutt's treatise *Specimens of Ancient Decorations from Pompeii* (published in 1825). Plaster finishes also played an important decorative role in many of the Historical-Revival interiors that appeared at various points throughout the 19th century.

Today, decorative painters continue the tradition of using antiqued frescoes on plaster walls to create a period atmosphere. For example, an earth-coloured scheme using locally available pigments would suit a wide range of country homes – from a villa in Tuscany, Italy, to a cottage in Cornwall, England, or a farmhouse in New Mexico. For a particularly Italian look the wall could also be polished to an alabaster-like sheen using either shellac or a proprietary acrylic resin and wax.

While decorating surfaces with fresco or fresco *secco* murals requires a degree of artistic skill and, in the case of "pure" fresco, specialist knowledge of how to apply paints and washes to wet plaster, it is nevertheless quite easy for the beginner to create a simple but highly effective simulation of the sort of plain fresco *secco* wall finish best associated with the vernacular architecture of the Mediterranean. The technique is demonstrated on pages 42-3, and includes instructions for a simple method of "ageing" the plaster.

Distressed plaster

Paints and Washes

A 1 part light blue powder pigment, 3 parts water.

B Powder pigment: 4 parts burnt sienna, 1 part burnt umber. Medium: 1 part white glue (PVA), 4 parts water. Ratios in wash: 1 part pigments, 9 parts medium.

A

B

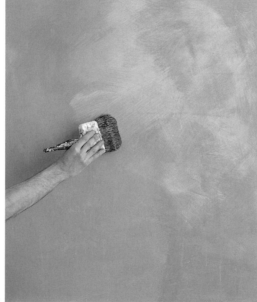

1

2

3

4

1 Using a large standard decorator's brush, apply two coats of pale blue paint A to a plaster wall pre-sealed with one coat of slightly thinned white latex (matte emulsion) paint. Allow to dry for four hours after each coat.

2 Seal the surface by brushing on a wash consisting of 3 parts white glue (PVA) to 2 parts water, and allow to dry for two hours.

3 Using a small standard decorator's brush, dab on a soft, untinted furniture wax in random patches over the surface. Increase the number and size of the patches according to how distressed you wish the finish to look.

4 Before the wax sets, mix up a batch of gypsum finishing plaster and apply a thin skim of it over the wall using a plasterer's float.

5 The plaster will start to dry almost as soon as it is applied, so gently brush a little water over the surface and smooth out any ridges with the float as quickly as possible.

6 After the plaster has dried (24-48 hours depending on room temperature) use a hammer or bolster to hit those areas of the wall where the wax was applied. As the plaster over these patches loosens and cracks, scrape it off with a steel spatula or wallpaper stripper to reveal the pale blue basecoat below.

8

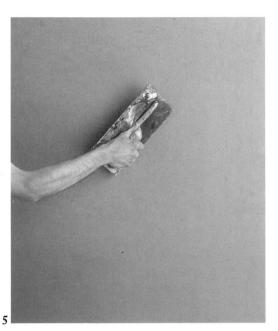

5

6

7

7 Using a coarse-grade sandpaper, smooth down the edges of the cracks and any surface abrasions made by the hammer or spatula. Then wipe down the wall with a clean rag to remove any plaster dust clinging to the surface.

8 Mix up orange-brown, white glue (PVA) wash B and brush it out roughly over the wall with a large decorator's brush to tint and seal the surface.

Milk paint

Above:
Milk (or casein) paint is applied directly to wood, dries to an opaque matte finish and, unlike many modern synthetic paints mellows pleasingly with age.

Prior to the end of the 19th century, pre-mixed pigments and paints were rarely available outside cities and other areas of high population. In North America, Europe and Scandinavia the painters and decorators who travelled between towns and villages plying their trade were therefore obliged to mix up paints and glazes on site, and augment the limited range of materials they carried with them with locally available ingredients. To meet the demand for painted joinery and furniture they used a variety of mediums, some of which proved more practical than others.

While limewash was effective for protecting and colouring walls made from traditional materials (*see* pages 32-34 and 168), it was less suitable for wooden panelling, doors and furniture. Limewash prepared from immature lime putty or mixed incorrectly tended to leave a chalky deposit on clothing when rubbed against.

Distemper, widely used for colourwashing interior walls (*see* pages 62-63 and 168), was also used to good effect to colour wood, particularly in Scandinavia. However, it also had a tendency to rub off over time, and could flake in damp conditions.

Egg *tempera*, an emulsion made by mixing pigment with linseed oil, water and egg yolk (the binding agent) was, on the other hand, exceptionally hard-wearing, and gave wooden surfaces a delicate, translucent veil of colour. However, it took a very long time to dry, was relatively expensive and therefore unsuitable for less wealthy clients.

Similarly, traditional oil paints – in common use in many areas from the 17th century onward – were hard-wearing, provided good opacity and rich, luminous colour, but were expensive. Moreover, the process of grinding pigment and mixing it with oil (usually linseed) was hard work and time-consuming for the painter.

For many painters, milk paint (buttermilk or casein paint) offered a good compromise between easily available, inexpensive ingredients, ease of preparation and application, durability and strength of colour. Made by mixing earth-coloured pigments with buttermilk or skimmed milk (readily available in

Right:
The door and wooden plank walls in the hallway of a Chester County, Amish log house of 1737 still boast their original Colonial-red milk paint finish.

44

Milk paint

agricultural communities) and a little lime (for its insecticidal and fungicidal properties), milk paint dries to a smooth, flat finish, offers a clarity of colour rarely found in modern synthetic paints, mellows with age and, unlike emulsion and oil-based paints, has a pleasant smell during application.

Particularly popular in North America during the late 18th and 19th centuries, milk paint is best associated with Colonial-style interiors. Examples of milk-painted furniture and other domestic artefacts can be seen at the Abby Aldrich Rockefeller Folk Art Center, near the Colonial Williamsburg Historic Area, in Virginia.

The milk paint colour swatches shown *left* were reproduced to match the colours found on protected areas – such as the undersides of lids and drawers – of artefacts in the museum. In other words, the colours were taken from areas least exposed to the ageing effects of light, dirt and grime, and therefore they appear as they would have looked when first applied, rather than with the patination of age as they do now.

If you are recreating a period interior, or seeking an attractive alternative to modern paints, various manufacturers in Britain and the United States produce lime and lead-free paints made to modern safety standards. A list of suppliers and manufacturers of pre-mixed milk paints can be found in the Directory.

Right:
The wooden panelling, fire surround and glazing bars in this American keeping room have been repainted with a Colonial-redmilk paint, colour-matched to traces of the original paintwork discovered during restoration.

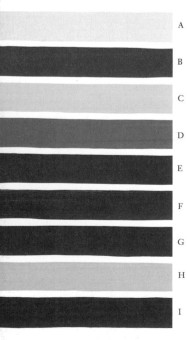

A

B

C

D

E

F

G

H

I

Milk Paints
Reproductions of colours found on 19th-century painted furniture in Williamsburg, Virginia:

A Pale yellow (chair)
B Rust (cupboard)
C Yellow (chair)
D Blue (clock)
E Bright red (rocking-horse)
F Green (chair)
G Reddish-brown (cupboard)
H Pale blue (dressing-table)
I Dark red (rocking-horse)

Right:

Home-made stencils of traditional motifs, irregularly spaced and applied in a single colour over a harmonious, earth-coloured ground-coat, look particularly effective in rustic interiors. The effect can be further enhanced if the internal edges of the stencil are imperfectly cut and the paint rubbed back with sandpaper.

Right:

This wall stencilling in a house in Devon, England, was copied from the stencilled bedroom at the American Museum in Bath, England. In North America during the 18th and for much of the 19th centuries, stencilling such as this provided an inexpensive alternative to costly, hand-printed wallpapers.

Stencilling

Stencilling, a method of transferring a motif or pattern onto a contrasting coloured background by applying paint through cut-outs in a stencil card, has its origins in very early cultures. The Chinese are credited with developing the art of stencilling around 3000 BC, discoveries of stencilled silks and paper in the Caves of the Thousand Buddhas, at Tunhuang in West China, having confirmed this. Similarly, there are many surviving examples of stencilled Egyptian artefacts (notably, mummy cases). Today, most stencils are cut from either oiled-card or clear acetate. Primitive cultures, however, used materials such as leather, leaves and wood. The Eskimos, for example, employed stencils cut from dried sealskins to decorate their clothing and homes, while natives of the Fijian islands applied vegetable dyes through the holes made by insects in banana and bamboo leaves.

In medieval Britain stencilling was largely confined to church interiors, their walls embellished with traditional heraldic symbols in red, green and gold-coloured pigments. Although faded, some of these ecclesiastical motifs have survived, and many reappeared later in the Gothic Revivalist's designs for wallpaper and tiles. In Tudor England stencilled wall-hangings of hessian were widely employed in grander dwellings, and unpanelled limewashed walls provided a background for hand-painted or stencilled patterns. While in France, stencilling was

popular as early as the Middle Ages and was used on textiles and books as well as in interiors.

It is interesting to note that as early as the 14th century the French had developed a technique for producing hand-blocked wall hangings which involved applying dusted, chopped wool onto sheets of handmade paper previously impressed and stencilled with rabbit glue. Unfortunately, due to damp and rodent and insect infestation in the average 14th-century household, few examples have survived. However, some 16th-century French papers, printed with small geometrical motifs, mostly black, then hand-stencilled and applied to items of furniture, have stood the test of time.

With the introduction of exquisite hand-painted wallpapers in Europe, particularly France and England, at the end of the 17th and throughout the 18th centuries, hand stencilling became less fashionable as a means of decorating entire walls in the homes of the wealthy. However, in Regency England it was common to see walls painted in flat, plain colours and augmented with borders (often simple Greek or Egyptian motifs) applied freehand or stencilled. Later, a feature of the splendours of High Victorian and Second Empire decorations was the embellishment of ceilings in grand reception rooms with stencilled garlands of flowers and fruit and rich polychromy. Moreover, where

48

Stencilling

Top right and middle right:
Various companies now produce printed stencilled wallpapers, many of which are copied from original 18th- and 19th-century stencil motifs and patterns. Some of the papers are available "pre-aged", the colours rubbed back to simulate the natural effects of exposure to light, dust and dirt and general wear and tear.

Bottom right:
The flower and leaf motif stencilling in the corner of this rustic interior was copied from original decorations *c.* 1800 found in Lower Dairy Farm, at Little Hocksley, England.

Far right:
Tom Hickman used a simple leaf motif stencil on the walls as a backdrop for his fine collection of provincial furniture and 19th-century pottery. The stencil was home-made and inspired by motifs displayed in St Fagan's Folk Art Museum, outside Cardiff in Wales. Hickman used a traditional green milk paint and, to give the motif a softer, time-worn look, applied it through the stencil cut-outs with a cotton ball, rather than with a stencilling brush.

Above:

The wooden plank walls of this cottage near Houston, Texas, were "pattern-box" stencilled by itinerant German painters at the end of the 19th century.

printed wallpapers or silks were not used, the stencil motifs were sometimes taken down the walls.

While the ever-increasing availability of wallpaper during the 18th and 19th centuries made hand-stencilled decorations either less desirable or, compared with mass-produced printed papers, uneconomic to some city and town dwellers, in rural areas it was a different matter. Wallpapers and silks were either too expensive, unsuitable for often damp wooden or plaster walls or, particularly in the case of the North American Colonies, simply not

available. In such communities stencilling was a form of folk art, a relatively cheap way of introducing colour and pattern into the home and imitating the wallpapered interiors of wealthier town and city houses.

Folk art stencilling was usually executed by itinerant artists and craftsmen. In North America many were of European extraction and brought with them ideas on decoration from their place of birth. The flamboyant stencilling in 17th-century Dutch and 18th-century Scandinavian interiors, for example, was reflected in the profusion of hand-stencilled motifs and patterns applied to walls, floors, joinery, furniture and artefacts in Colonial interiors. Applied with milk paint or distemper, the stencilled motifs and patterns were inspired by nature; garlands of fruit, flowers, leaves and berries and images of animals and birds were popular.

Above:

This repeat-pattern stencil frieze was uncovered by carefully scrubbing off subsequently applied layers of paint during the restoration of the room.

It is the versatility and engaging simplicity of stencilling that has both ensured its survival and seen it flourish as a decorative technique from the late 19th century to the present day. For example, it played an important role in the works of both William Morris and William Burges – the latter, influenced by medieval artists, making extensive use of the technique, notably in rooms at Castle Coch and on some of the furniture he designed. Stencilling also featured strongly in many Art Nouveau interiors in which walls were divided by richly coloured stencilled bands,

augmented with friezes of long-stemmed flowers and stylized birds. (One of the finest examples of stencilled wall panelling from this period can be seen at Charles Rennie Mackintosh's tea rooms in Glasgow, Scotland.) While in North America, Louis Comfort Tiffany used stencilling not only on glass,

but also for the decoration of private client's interiors and on public buildings erected during the 1920s and 1930s.

A great boon to the would-be stenciller today is the ready availability of an enormous range of pre-cut stencils in traditional motifs and patterns (for the names and addresses of suppliers, refer to the Directory, pages 172-175). However, for those who would prefer to design and cut their own stencils, step-by-step instructions and accompanying illustrations are provided under Folk Art Stencilling, on pages 54-55.

Milk Paints

A Pale yellow
buttermilk paint.
B Dark green
buttermilk paint.
C Bright red
buttermilk paint.

Folk art stencil

The technique shown here for copying and cutting-out a one-piece stencil of a traditional American folk art leaf motif can be adapted to almost any other relatively simple pattern. If your source material isn't to the scale you require, and you don't feel confident enough to copy it free-hand (as has been done in the illustration here), it can be easily enlarged or reduced to size accordingly on a suitable photo-copier before tracing off. Similarly, the technique shown for repeating the stencil vertically down a wall can also be adapted to create horizontal borders across a wall.

1 Using a sheet of tracing paper and a pencil, either trace directly from source material or, as here, draw freehand the outlines of the leaf pattern and border.

2 Reverse the paper and, using diagonal strokes, rub over the back of it with a stick of graphite.

3 Turn over the paper, so that the graphite shading is on the underside, and attach it with masking tape to a sheet of oiled stencil card. Position the paper so that the tops of the border leaves are 3mm below the top edge of the card. Then, pressing firmly, pencil around the outlines of the leaf pattern to transfer them to the stencil card below.

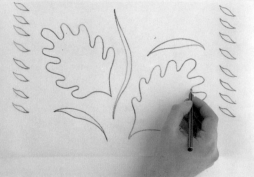

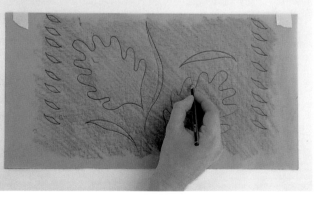

4 Remove the tracing paper and cut out the leaf pattern from the card with a scalpel or craft knife. A good tip when cutting along a curve is to turn the card around the blade, rather than the blade around the card. This will minimize the risk of the blade slipping, and thus cutting off line (or cutting your fingers!).

5 Use low-tack masking tape to secure the stencil card in position at the top of a wall pre-painted with two coats of pale yellow milk paint A. Check the card is vertically and horizontally true with a spirit-level.

   Dip a small marine sponge into a saucer of dark green milk paint (B), removing excess paint by dabbing the sponge on lining paper. (Failure to do this may result in paint running down behind the card.) Then gently dab the sponge over the green leaf cut-outs, working on one leaf at a time.

   Subtle shadows can be created by building up layers of paint; highlights by applying fewer layers, or diluting the paint with a little water.

6 Having completed the green leaves, employ the technique used in step 5 with bright red milk paint C to stencil in the red leaves. After the paint has dried (this will take approximately four hours), carefully remove the stencil and clean off any paint smears that may have crept onto the back of it with a damp lint-free rag.

7 Darken paints B and C by adding a little burnt umber powder pigment to both of them and, using a fine artist's brush, apply darker shadows along those edges of the leaves furthest from the predominant light source. This will give the stencil more of a three-dimensional quality. Then allow the surface to dry for up to four hours.

5

6

8 To repeat the pattern down the wall, tape the card in position directly underneath the completed stencil. (The gap between the top edge of the card and the bottom of the border leaves above it equals the gap between any two leaves minus 3mm.) Then, having checked the card is vertically and horizontally true, repeat steps 5-7.

(Repeat steps 5-8 until you reach the bottom of the wall. Parallel bands of leaves can be applied as desired.)

9 Once the paint has dried you can age the surface by rubbing it down with a medium-grade sandpaper. Work in long vertical, diagonal and horizontal sweeps, applying an even pressure throughout.

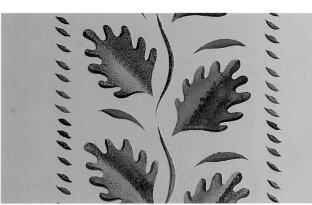

7

8

9

Above:
A somewhat strident sponged wall finish, achieved by applying two red and one off-white oil-based glaze with a small marine sponge, provides the backdrop to a brace of 18th- and 19th-century wooden artefacts.

Broken colour

Many period finishes and effects are created by using techniques that have their origins in fine art. Nowadays, we know them as broken colour techniques – that is, methods of distressing a semi-translucent paint or glaze, applied over a contrasting-coloured, opaque groundcoat, to produce patterns and subtle gradations of colour over a surface. The effects are either aesthetically pleasing in their own right, or a replication of a natural material, such as wood or marble, or a simulation of a naturally occurring chemical process, such as the "breakdown" of pigments in many traditional paints.

Colourwashing (*see* pages 62-3) involves applying thin washes of glaze over a groundcoat in order to build up subtle veils of colour over a surface. Usually, no effort is made to disguise brushmarks as they give the finish additional pattern, texture and body.

Ragging (*see* page 65) involves brushing out a glaze over an opaque groundcoat and then dabbing it with a loosely bunched rag, moistened with solvent, to remove patches of glaze. The result is an attractive randomly patterned finish that simulates traditional flat-painted surfaces that have become mottled due to pigment breakdown.

Right:
A stone fire surround provides the focal point in this 19th-century Gothick hallway. Dragged joinery, ragged, dragged and spattered walls and a *trompe l'oeil* cornice play essential supporting roles.

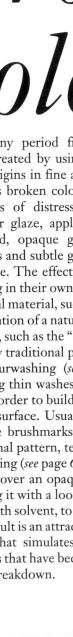

Sponging involves dabbing a marine sponge, moistened with solvent, over wet water- or oil-based glazes to create a random, speckled pattern. The technique can be used to create *faux* stone finishes (*see* Stoneblocking, page 119).

Combing involves dragging a comb cut from oiled-card, plastic or steel through a wet glaze to produce vertical, horizontal or wavy stripes that allow the groundcoat to ghost through. Decorators use the technique to simulate figuring in fantasy woodgrains (*see* Woodgraining, pages 93-105).

Dragging involves pulling the bristles of a dragging brush down through a wet glaze in a series of parallel motions to produce a uniformly striped finish, particularly on joinery, that is aesthetically pleasing in its own right and also used for the simulation of woodgrains (*see* pages 93-105).

Stippling involves tapping the bristle tips of a stippling brush or a hog's hair softener over a wet glaze to either disguise brushmarks left in it during application, or blend different glazes together to create subtle shading and gradations of colour.

Spattering involves flicking flecks of wet glaze at random over an opaque groundcoat to create an overlay of specks of colour. The technique is used to simulate insect infestation in painted or varnished joinery (*see* Antiquing, page 73, and Dusty paint, pages 78-9), or stones such as porphyry and granite (*see* Stonework, page 114).

Cissing involves spattering flecks of solvent over a wet glaze (mineral spirits/white spirit on oil-based glazes, water or acetic acid on water-based paints and glazes). The solvent disperses the glaze to form a ring in which the underlying groundcoat ghosts through the middle and tonal gradations appear on the circumference. The technique is used in Bird's eye maple graining (*see* pages 104-5) and, like the spattering technique already discussed, to simulate fossil forms in *faux* stone and marble.

Softening and blending involves gently brushing the bristle tips of a badger or hog's hair softener over wet glazes to blend them together or into the background. The technique is used in Marbling (*see* pages 106-113) and to simulate a Nicotine finish (*see* page 66).

Finally, wiping out involves removing areas of wet glaze from a surface with a rag to allow the underlying groundcoat to ghost through. The technique is used in Antiquing (*see* page 73) and for creating highlights on raised mouldings (*see* Dusty paint, pages 78-9) and embossed wallpapers such as Lincrusta (*see* pages 154-5).

Far left:
The walls of this 1850s sitting room have been colour-washed in two shades of yellow. The cornice was painted with a yellow glaze and gently wiped with a rag to create highlights on the raised sections of the moulding.

Top left:
The walls of this 18th-century French-style interior were decorated by sparsely brushing coloured glaze over a white gesso groundcoat and then pulling a comb vertically through the still-wet glaze to produce a subtle dragged effect.

Middle left:
The walls of this 14th-century English farmhouse have been colour-washed in ochre and Indian red.

Bottom left:
A wall and dado in the Sir John Soane Museum, London, England, ragged and spattered to create a fantasy *faux* porphyry effect.

Overleaf:
The two-colour ragged wall finish in this Georgian-style Park Avenue apartment in New York simulates the chemical breakdown of pigments that often took place in paints after they had been applied.

A

B

Paints and Glazes

A Pale gray eggshell subtly tinted with small quantities of lilac, blue and red artist's oils.

B Pigments: 8 parts white eggshell paint and 1 part alizarin crimson and 1 part ultramarine artist's oil. Medium: 3 parts transparent oil glaze, 1 part mineral spirits (white spirit). Ratios in glaze: 1 part pigments, 12 parts medium.

1

2

Colourwashing

Traditionally, distemper was used for colourwashing walls. However, the two examples of the finish shown here employ modern water- and oil-based paints because they offer better coverage and durability while still producing authentic-looking results. Beyond copying these examples, you are advised to experiment with alternative colour combinations on suitably primed lining paper.

1 Onto a previously primed and undercoated wall apply one or two coats of pale gray paint A, using a large standard decorator's brush. Allow each coat to dry for 24 hours.

2 Again using a large standard decorator's brush, apply one coat of lilac glaze B. Brush the glaze roughly over the surface in all directions, allowing the underlying gray to ghost through the lilac at random.

3

3 As you can see, no attempt should be made to disguise the brushmarks during step 2, as they are essential to the casual appearance and authenticity of the finish. If desired, once the surface has dried thoroughly a coat of clear matte water-based varnish can be applied for protection.

1

2

3

4

1 Onto a previously
primed and
undercoated wall,
apply one or two
coats of pale blue
paint A. Allow
each coat to dry
for roughly three or
four hours.

2 Using a large
standard decorator's
brush, apply one
coat of mid-blue
glaze B. As with the
gray and lilac
colourwash shown
opposite, roughly
brush the glaze in
all directions over
the surface, allowing
the underlying pale
blue to ghost
through at random,
and making no
attempt to disguise
the brushmarks.
Then leave the
surface to dry for up
to four hours.

3 Repeat step 2
using dark blue
glaze C.

4 As you can see,
the application of a
second colourwash
produces a cloudier,
less brushy finish
than a single
colourwash (as
opposite).
   Water-based
eggshell provides a
fairly durable finish.
However, surfaces
likely to be subject
to excessive wear
and tear can be
given a coat of clear
matte polyurethane
varnish for extra
protection.

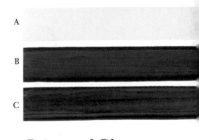

Paints and Glazes
A Pale blue, water-
based eggshell paint.
B 1 part mid-blue,
water-based eggshell
paint, 1 part water.
C 3 parts dark blue,
water-based eggshell
paint, 1 part water.

2 Again using a standard decorator's brush, apply one coat of glaze B. Don't worry about leaving brush marks in the glaze.

3 Working quickly, lightly brush a badger softener in all directions over the wet surface to soften and blend the glaze and disguise the brushmarks.

4 Make up a crumpled pad from a lint-free cotton rag, and lightly dab it over the wet surface to remove irregular-shaped patches of glaze. Keep reforming the pad, and replace the rag when it becomes clogged with glaze.

Note: Depending upon the room temperature, you have about half–an–hour to distress the glaze with the rag before it starts to become unworkable.

5 Leave the surface to dry for roughly 24 hours, and then apply one or two coats of matte, satin or gloss clear water-based varnish for protection.

Left:
As part of the recreation of this period interior, the walls have been ragged in shades of yellow – simulating the "streaking" caused by unstable pigments in many traditional paints.

1

2

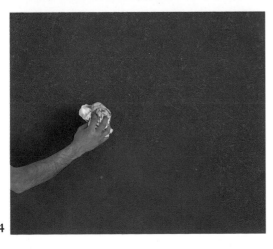

3

4

5

1 Using a standard decorator's brush, apply two coats of terracotta paint A to the previously primed and undercoated surface. Allow 24 hours drying time after each coat.

A

B

Ragging

In the example shown here, the ragged finish is created by distressing an oil-based glaze with a clean, lint-free cotton rag. However, variations in pattern and texture can be produced by using the same technique and rags made from materials as diverse as hessian, muslin, silk and even polythene or plastic.

Note: Because of the fairly rapid drying time, when applying this finish to large surface areas, such as walls, it is recommended that one person brushes on and softens the glaze, while another follows behind distressing with the rag.

Paints and Glazes

A Terracotta colour eggshell paint.
B Artist's oils: 6 parts burnt sienna, 1 part alizarin crimson.
Medium: 3 parts transparent oil glaze, 2 parts mineral spirits (white spirit). Ratios in glaze: 1 part pigments, 8 parts medium.

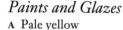

A

B

Nicotine

1

2

Paints and Glazes

A Pale yellow eggshell paint.
B Artist's oils: 3 parts burnt sienna, 4 parts burnt umber.
Medium: 3 parts transparent oil glaze, 2 parts mineral spirits (white spirit). Ratios in glaze: 1 part pigment, 30 parts medium.

Right:
A dry-brushing technique has been used on the door, walls and ceiling of this country kitchen to simulate the texture and discolouration of ageing paint. Natural blackening of the ceiling from candles will accentuate the effect.

As with ragging (see page 65), the glaze used for nicotine dries fairly rapidly. Consequently, when decorating large surface areas such as ceilings and walls it is strongly recommended that two people share the workload: the first brushing on the glaze, the second stippling it, and the first softening and blending it – all while it is still wet and therefore workable.

1 Using a standard decorator's brush, apply two coats of pale yellow paint A to the previously primed and undercoated surface. Leave to dry overnight after each coat.

2 Roughly brush out yellow glaze B over the surface, using a short-bristled standard decorator's brush.

3 Working as quickly as you can, remove the brushmarks and create a textured, dappled effect in the wet glaze by dabbing and stippling it with the bristle tips of a dusting brush. As you work, keep wiping the brush on a clean rag to remove the build-up of glaze on the bristles.

4 Again working as quickly as you can, lightly brush a badger softener in all directions over the wet glaze to soften and blend it, creating a cloudy effect with subtle gradations of depth and colour across the surface.

5 Leave the surface to dry for approximately 24 hours and then, if desired, apply a coat of satin or gloss finish clear polyurethane varnish for protection. (The varnish will also lend a greater sense of depth to the finish.)

3

4

Ageing paint

Above left:

Like many similar pieces, this simple country dresser remains more valuable with its original (distressed) paintwork left intact, than if it had been stripped to the bare wood.

Above right:

Five layers of paint were scraped off the panelling in this 18th-century Rhode Island room to reveal the original finish below.

*P*ainted period furniture and joinery almost inevitably displays signs of ageing after exposure to light, damp, dust, dirt and general wear and tear over the years. Once pristine, paintwork will fade, darken, flake or craze, and posssibly be chipped or scuffed, depending upon the conditions under which it is kept and the degree to which it is cared for. The fact that the paintwork on an 18th- or 19th-century provincial chest of drawers or chair may be "damaged" does not necessarily make it unpleasant to look at. Indeed, the patination of age is often aesthetically pleasing and may well add to the value of the piece of furniture in question. It is not surprising, therefore, that painters and decorators have stolen a march on time and devised various ingenious techniques for artificially ageing new paintwork.

One of the simpler methods for ageing paint is to apply an oil-based antiquing glaze consisting of, for example, artist's oils, such as burnt umber, Van Dyke brown and black, suspended in a clear medium of transparent oil glaze (scumble) and mineral spirits (white spirit). The glaze darkens the surface of the paint, simulating the dirt and grime that naturally becomes embedded in the surface over the years. To increase the "authenticity" of the effect, greater concentrations of glaze are applied to the recesses of mouldings – in other words, those areas where you would expect more dirt and grime to accumulate. Conversely, raised sections of mouldings are wiped down with a rag to leave the barest trace of glaze on the paint. Additional signs of ageing can, of course, be created by spattering small flecks of glaze at random over the surface in order to simulate the presence of insect infestation, such as woodworm. (A technique for applying an antiquing glaze is shown on page 73.)

Another simple but effective technique for ageing paintwork is to rub it down with sandpaper or steel (wire) wool. Gently done, this will lighten the colour and simulate the effects of exposure to light. For a more "authentic" finish, some thought should be given to composition – areas exposed to direct sunlight will have faded more than those in the shade. Heavy rubbing back with a coarse grade paper or wool may well expose underlying coats of

Right:

This late 18th-century Canadian table, accompanying chairs and fruit bowl are a delightful example of the attraction of a time-worn painted finish in a rustic interior. The doors behind were painted in harmonious colours and then judiciously sanded down to simulate the unpredictable effects of exposure to moisture and wear and tear.

Right:
The plank walls, doors and architrave in this late 19th-century cottage were colourwashed by itinerant German painters in the 1870s. The original colours were discovered intact under layers of paint during a recent restoration.

Right:
In another room in the cottage shown *left* a contrasting mid-brown paint was applied to the bottom layers of planking to simulate a dado/skirting board (baseboard) and, at the same time, visually "reduce" the height of the room.

contrasting-coloured primer. As a simulation of heavy wear and tear this is best done with discretion, and restricted to more exposed areas, such as the architrave around doorways and raised sections of mouldings on furniture. (The technique for rubbing down is included in the instructions for producing a dusty paint finish, on page 79, and a flaking paint result, on pages 74-5.)

One characteristic of paint, particularly an oil-based type, is that it will flake off if there is moisture in the underlying wood, or if it is regularly exposed to a humid atmosphere (such as in a kitchen). New paintwork can be encouraged to flake immediately after application by dabbing patches of wax at random over the underlying groundcoat. Any coat of paint applied over the top will fail to adhere to the wax, and can then be flaked up by gentle rubbing with the steel blade of a wallpaper scraper or spatula. (The technique for creating a flaking paint effect is shown on pages 74-5).

Another characteristic of painted or varnished surfaces is that they have a tendency to crack and craze over time as the underlying wood expands and contracts according to the rise and fall in humidity and temperature. A method of simulating this process was developed in France as long ago as the 18th century. The technique involves applying two coats of proprietary *craquelure* (crackle) varnish over the painted surface. The second coat is applied approximately one hour after the first coat (or when the latter has become tacky). Because the first coat has started to dry, and therefore is contracting at a faster rate than the second one, it pulls the top coat apart, causing fine cracks and crazing to appear in the surface. Once the varnish has dried, a tinted glaze is then rubbed into and wiped off the surface. The glaze remains in the cracks and thus defines the intricate pattern of crazing over the surface of the paint. (A technique for applying crackle varnish is shown on pages 76-7.)

1

2

1 Key the varnished
surface of the
mahogany door (*see*
pages 99-101) with
00 steel wool,
wiping off any debris
with a clean rag.

Left:
Paintwork flaked
off, rubbed down
and discoloured to
simulate various
degrees of ageing.

2 Using a 1in
(2.5cm) artist's
brush, apply glaze A
to the moulding and
perimeter area of
the middle panel.

3 Make a flat pad of
clean dry rag and
wipe off most of the
glaze from the panel
and raised sections
of the moulding,
leaving behind an

3

5

Antiquing

6

The application of a dirty brown oil-based glaze – illustrated here on a mahogany-grained door – is a traditional and versatile method of artificially ageing furniture, architectural features such as picture rails, dados and skirtings, and papered and painted walls and ceilings. As a simulation of the dust and dirt that naturally accumulates over the passing years, it is most effective when sympathetically applied to the recesses of mouldings and embossed surfaces – in other words, those areas least exposed to light and most prone to the accumulation of grime.

A

4

accumulation of glaze in the recesses and at the edges of the moulding.

4 To simulate worm holes and any natural discolouration, charge an angled fitch with a little of glaze A, wiping any excess off onto a piece of paper.

Then, holding the brush approximately 6ins (15cms) above the door, pull a forefinger through the bristles to send a fine spatter of glaze over the surface.

Note: To help you develop control of the spattering technique you are advised to practise it

a few times on a spare piece of lining paper, before attempting it on the door.

5 Repeat the spattering at random over the surface, but for authenticity don't

overdo it. Remove overly-large spots of glaze with a rag dampened with mineral spirits (white spirit).

6 Finally, the door can be given a coat of clear satin or gloss polyurethane varnish for extra protection.

Glaze
A Artist's oils: 1 part Van Dyke brown, 1 part black. Medium: transparent oil glaze. Ratios in glaze: 3 parts artist's oils to 1 part medium.

1

2

3

4

Flaking paint

Paints and Glazes

A Pale cream eggshell paint.

B Powder pigments: 2 parts raw sienna, 2 parts raw umber, 2 parts white latex (matte emulsion) paint, 1 part black. Medium: water. Ratios in glaze: 1 part pigments, 1 part water.

C 3 parts cherry red latex (matte emulsion) paint, 2 parts black powder pigment.

D 3 parts poppy red latex (matte emulsion) paint, 3 parts white latex (matte emulsion) paint, 2 parts burnt sienna powder pigment.

E 3 parts poppy red latex (matte emulsion) paint, 2 parts burnt sienna powder pigment.

F 1 part burnt umber powder pigment, 1 part water.

1 Brush on two coats of paint A, allowing each one to dry overnight. Then, following steps 2-4 of oak graining (*see* pages 102-3), use glaze B to lightly grain the door and, again, leave to dry overnight.

2 Using an artist's brush, apply small patches of a soft wax to those areas where you would like subsequent coats of paint to flake off.

3 Following the direction of the grain, apply one coat of paint C, using a 2in (5cm) standard decorator's brush, and leave to dry for four hours.

4 Repeat step 3 using paint D, and again allow to dry for four hours.

5 Repeat steps 3-4 using paint E and a dry-brushing technique: dip the bristles of an old standard decorator's brush into paint E, wipe off most of the paint onto a piece of lining paper, and then lightly brush what's left sparingly over the door, allowing streaks of the underlying paler colour to grin through. Then leave to dry for roughly two hours.

6 Using a steel spatula, carefully scrape over the areas where you applied the wax. The layers of paint will flake off to reveal the underlying graining.

7 Working in the direction of the underlying grain, rub down the surface with a medium-grade sandpaper. Rub harder over sharp edges and sections you would expect to be naturally subject to the greatest wear and tear – cutting back the top coat to reveal either of the two underlying

5

6

7

8

9

coats, or even more of the graining. You can also, as here, extend the areas of flaking. In other areas, simply rub gently with a fine-grade sandpaper to soften and fade the top coat.

8 To further age the surface, brush on a coat of antiquing glaze F. Build up the glaze in the recesses around the middle panel – where you would expect to find the greatest accumulation of dirt and grime. Leave to dry for roughly four hours.

9 Finally, brush on a coat of matte, satin or gloss clear polyurethane varnish for protection.

Paints and Glazes

A **Black oil (gloss) paint.**

B **4 parts cadmium red artist's oil, 1 part transparent oil glaze.**

The craquelure technique shown here can be used to simulate fine cracks and crazing often found in old varnished surfaces, notably on pieces of furniture, panelling and ceramics. However, it is not recommended on large surface areas, such as walls, because of the considerable difficulty of carefully laying off two coats of rapidly drying crackle varnish without leaving ugly brush marks that would ruin the look of the finish.

1

Craquelure

1 Onto a previously primed and mid-gray undercoated surface, apply two coats of black paint A with a standard decorator's brush. Allow the surface to dry for roughly 24 hours after each coat.

2 Using a fine-bristled varnishing brush, apply one coat of crackle varnish. Allow the surface to dry until it becomes tacky (roughly one hour). Then carefully apply a second coat of varnish.

2

3

4

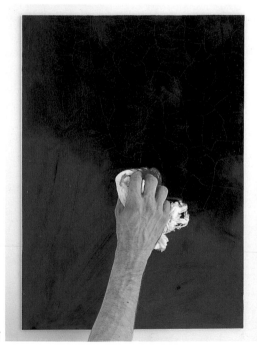

5

3 After roughly half-an-hour fine cracks or crazing will begin to appear over the surface as the two coats, drying at different rates, pull each other apart. The size of the cracks depends on the thickness of the coats of varnish – the thicker the coats the larger the cracks.

4 Leave for roughly one hour, then carefully brush on a coat of red glaze B.

5 Using a clean, dry, lint-free rag, folded to form a flat-faced pad, wipe off most of the glaze from the surface. Keep reforming the pad so that you don't wipe the glaze back onto the surface again.

The glaze will remain in the cracks, thus defining the intricate pattern of crazing across the surface established in steps 2-3. Again, allow the surface to dry for roughly 24 hours.

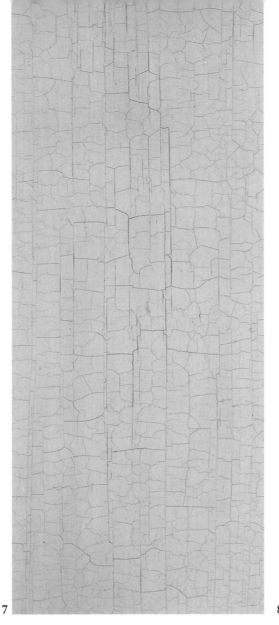

7

8

6

6 Once again using the varnishing brush, apply one or two coats of satin or gloss finish clear polyurethane varnish for protection, allowing approximately 24 hours drying time between coats.

7 This craquelure finish was achieved using the same method as for the black and red, by substituting a beige-coloured eggshell paint in step 1, and by using burnt umber to make up the glaze brushed on and wiped off in steps 4 and 5.

8 To create this craquelure variation the same method was employed again, but a sage green eggshell was used in step 1, thicker coats of crackle varnish were applied in step 2 (to increase the size of the crazing), and white eggshell, tinted with a little burnt umber, made up the glaze used in steps 4 and 5.

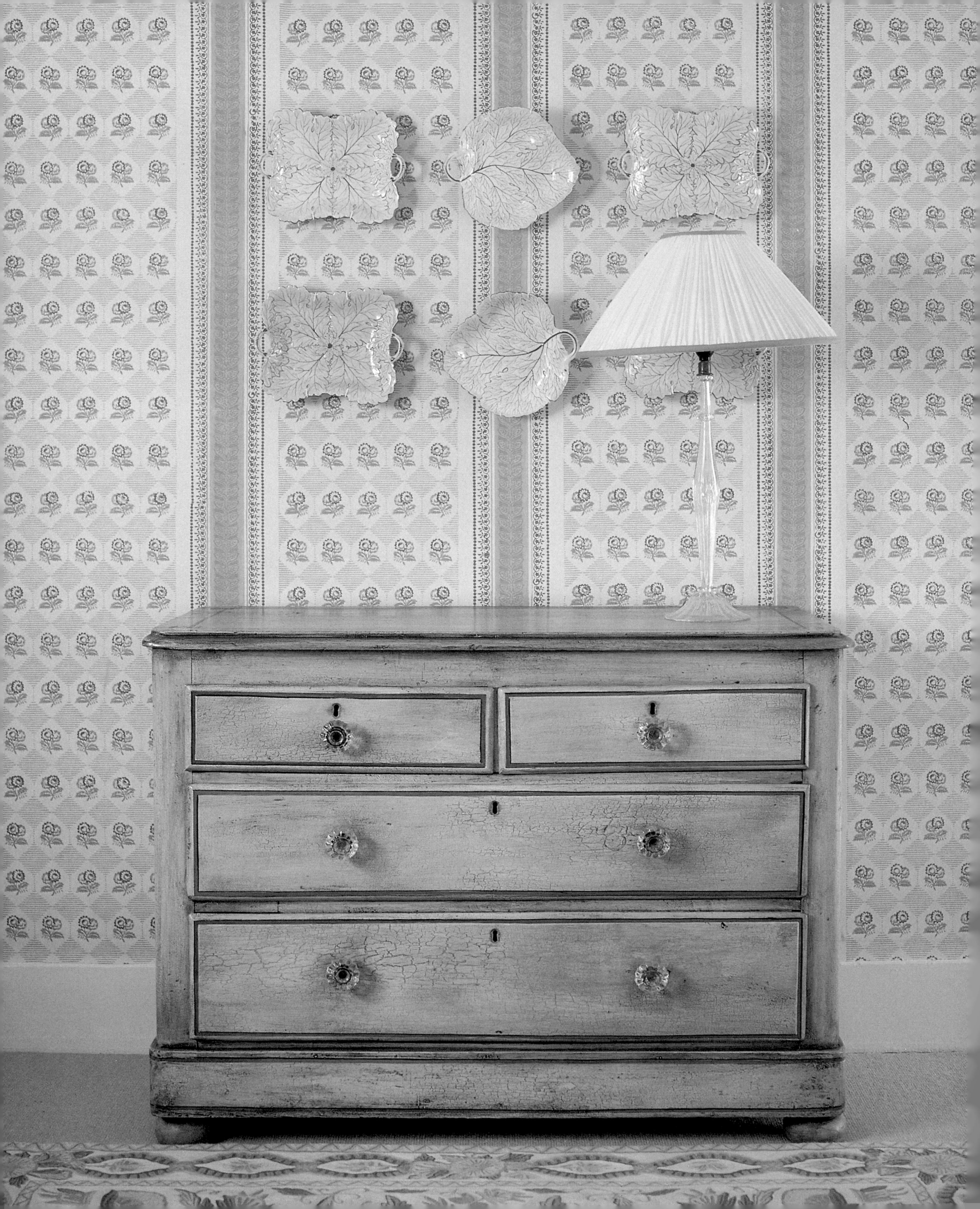

1

2

Left: **Dry-brushed, crackled and rubbed-back paintwork mimics the effects of ageing.**

Although illustrated here on a dado rail, the dusty paint finish can be successfully applied to items of furniture – especially simple country pieces such as chests of drawers, cupboards and linen presses – to give them an aged, rustic appearance.

3

Dusty paint

1 In this example, two coats of a pale yellow latex (matte emulsion) paint were applied to the wall above the dado, and two coats of a dark green eggshell paint to the Lincrusta below it. (Pre-seal the Lincrusta with a coat of primer.)

Having applied two coats of white latex (matte emulsion) paint to the dado itself, use a dry 1in (2.5 cm) decorator's brush to apply one coat of gray-green glaze A to the rail. Leave to dry for four hours.

2 Again using a dry decorator's brush, apply one coat of pale gray glaze B to the dado. Brush it out thinly over the surface so that random streaks and patches of the gray-green glaze below show through. Again, allow the surface to dry for approximately four hours.

3 Soften and blend the gray-green and pale gray glazes on the raised sections of the dado by gently rubbing them down with a medium-grade sandpaper. Wipe off any surface debris with a clean rag.

4 Apply one coat of antiquing glaze C to the rail. Leave to dry for two hours.

5 Protect the wall and Lincrusta with low-tack masking tape. Then add a little burnt umber powder pigment to glaze C to darken it. Charge the bristles of an old toothbrush or an angled fitch with the glaze and, holding the brush approximately 4ins (10cms) from the surface, draw a forefinger through the bristles to send a fine spatter of glaze over the rail. (Practise this technique first on a spare piece of lining paper.)

4

5

Paints and Glazes

A Pigments: 3 parts black powder pigment, 1 part emerald green latex (matte emulsion) paint, 6 parts white latex (matte emulsion) paint. Medium: water. Ratios in glaze: 4 parts pigments, 1 part water.

B 1 part glaze C above, 1 part white latex (matte emulsion) paint.

C Powder pigment: burnt umber. Medium: 1 part white

glue (PVA), 3 parts water. Ratios in glaze: 1 part pigment, 3 parts medium.

6 The spots of glaze should be neither too large nor too numerous. Remove any overly-large blobs with a damp rag.

A

B

C

6

Ageing wood

Above left:
**New pine plank
walls contrast with a
plank bench,
naturally weathered
after years outside
on a porch.**

Above right:
**Naturally aged
plank walls provide
an harmonious
backdrop for a
milk-painted
Pennsylvanian pine
cupboard (*c.* 1750)
and a poplar dry
sink (*c.* 1810)
displaying traces of
its original milk-
paint finish.**

*E*xposed to the atmosphere and general wear and tear, wooden surfaces will, in time, begin to exhibit various signs of ageing. For example, a piece of furniture exposed to sunlight will naturally lighten in colour as the sun "bleaches" its surface. On the other hand, an accumulation of dust, dirt and grime in a polished wooden surface darkens the original colour. Exposure to heat may also have an effect, particularly on veneered furniture; the expansion and contraction of the wood as it heats up and cools down causing the veneer to crack and lift off the base wood underneath. Insect infestation will also produce changes in the appearance of wood, woodworm and deathwatch beetle, for example, producing small holes in its surface and possibly even damaging the structural integrity of the piece. Damage caused by human intervention also plays a part in the ageing process. For example, table tops may well become scorched by hot wax from overturned candles and dents, scratches and gouges may appear as a result of careless handling of knives and forks, china and pots and pans, while table legs may become scuffed by careless feet.

Damage such as this is all part of the patination of age that naturally accumulates over time on furniture and joinery. The fact that it can be both aesthetically pleasing and confer an air of antiquity (and sometimes value, especially on furniture) to the object in question has meant that craftsmen have devised various methods for simulating the ageing process on new wood. For example, during the 19th century, oak beams and other woodwork was blackened with dark wood stains, as was the woodwork in houses built to the early 20th-century English "Tudorbethan" and American Tudor and Spanish Colonial-Revival styles. The intention was to create an "olde-worlde"

Right:
**Parham House, in
Sussex, England,
boasts an excellent
example of naturally
aged Elizabethan
oak wall panelling.
Years of waxing and
exposure to light
and dust have
turned the originally
pale wood a glorious
honey colour, which
is in sharp contrast
to the darker, and
sometimes
overpowering,
stained and waxed
or varnished wood
usually favoured in
the 19th century.**

80

decorative effect, rather than to deceive the onlooker into thinking that this was original 15th- or 16th-century woodwork. However, some 19th-century manufacturers of revival furniture probably had more dubious reasons for ageing their reproductions. Indeed, records show that some craftsmen of the time complained that pieces had to be "stained to imitate old, and sold for old".

From the 1870s, with the arrival of the Queen Anne revival style, it became acceptable for English and American houses to be furnished with antiques. Because the style was informal, even faded or worn pieces of furniture were not scorned. And it was only one step on from this fashion for manufacturers to start creating new antiques with a faded patina. In Europe, however, furnishing in period style was generally confined to reproduction pieces that were left looking sleek and new.

All manner of wooden surfaces can be artificially aged to harmonize with a period decorative scheme – furniture, picture frames, wall panelling, balustrades and handrails on stairs, for example, as well as floorboards and other joinery.

The importance of ageing wood in a period setting can be seen if you consider how the brand-new appearance of freshly installed floorboards or stair spindles will stand out against the time-worn surfaces around them, as will a new piece of wood used to repair an item of antique furniture.

However, your starting point should be to determine whether the wood would ever have been exposed in the first place. In the 1970s and 1980s many internal and external doors were stripped and then treated with coloured wax to mellow them. But unless the doors were made from fine woods, such as mahogany or oak, they were never intended to be left unpainted. If your doors are made of a softwood such as pine, you should consider repainting them.

Once you have determined that the wood should be on show, prepare the surface for treatment by sealing any knots (see p.171). You will not need to smooth the surface or use filler as any dents and cracks will only add to the distressed effect.

There are several methods of ageing brash new wood to blend it in with its surroundings and tone down its colour. One of the commonest is to rub over the wood with an antiquing glaze (see p.73), tinted with burnt umber, Vandyke brown or black artists' oils. This will simulate the effect of the gradual build-up of dirt and dust on a surface.

When applying the glaze, bear in mind that different areas of the piece will be dirtied at different rates. For example, grime will accumulate around the handle or pull areas on doors or drawers, while scuff marks will feature on the legs of a piece, near ground level. To create an authentic effect, you can try using a small paintbrush or child's toothbrush to work extra glaze into deep mouldings. Once you have applied the glaze, it will need to be treated with a protective varnish (see p.168-9).

Insect damage such as the exit holes left by woodworm or beetle larvaes can be simulated with the point of a compass or a nail. If you then rub a tinted wax or glaze into the exposed edges of the resulting holes, they will not look too pristine and will blend in with the surrounding surface. Before you begin to puncture your wood, you should examine wormy pieces to determine an authentic distribution of the holes.

An antiquing wax can be used to polish a new piece and speed up the build-up of patina. You can either buy a ready-tinted wax or you can make your own by mixing beeswax polish with either artists' colours or boot polish in order to tint it. Rub the wax well into the wood, leave for between 5 and 10 minutes, then rub off the excess and polish with a soft, lint-free cloth.

Oak can be "fumed" to darken it, in the manner of the late Arts and Crafts furniture makers. The wood is exposed to the fumes of ammonia after construction. Ammonia fumes are very dangerous, so this is a job for a specialist.

Other forms of damage can be simulated by distressing the wood. Techniques for this range from simply using sandpaper or steel wool to roughen the surface and lighten the colouring of the wood, through scrubbing the surface with a wire brush in order to open up the grain, to causing actual damage to the surface by hitting it vigorously with bicycle chains or hammers!

For a sun-bleached effect, an application of bleach or lime paste will draw the colour out of the wood effectively. Many floors and table tops were bleached and worn by daily scrubbing. For example, floorboards in pre-19th century homes were invariably left bare and unpolished. They were cleaned by regular scrubbing, sometimes using sand as a scouring agent. This effect can be imitated by brushing over a white emulsion or latex paint (for technique, see p.91). Since the floorboards were originally unpolished, however, you should avoid using a gloss varnish to seal the result; a matte-finish plyurethane varnish will give the best effect.

Above and below:
There are various ways of artificially ageing new floorboards. In the example *above* the pine floor has been treated with a green woodstain and then gently rubbed down with medium- and fine-grade sandpapers to dull and soften the finish and simulate wear and tear. In the example *below* a pale brown woodstain has been applied, and then rubbed down to produce a similar effect.

Right:
The original pine floorboards of an 18th-century barn in New York State have naturally darkened with age. Similarly, the small table displays the subtle patination that accrues over the years as a result of waxing and polishing and the accumulation of embedded dust and grime. (The barn's structural timbers and plank walls have been woodwashed in a contrasting pale mauve colour.)

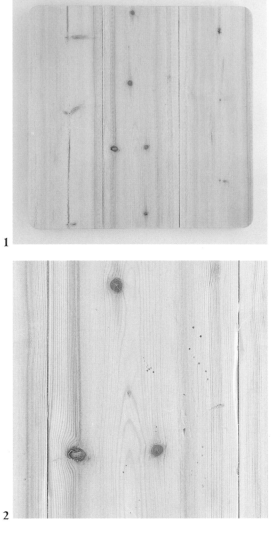

1 If the wooden surface has been previously sealed with varnish or lacquer, remove this with a commercial stripper, steel (wire) wool and a clean rag – making sure you carefully follow the instructions on the container. Allow to dry thoroughly, and then seal any knots with clear shellac (or clear knotting compound).

2 Evidence of woodworm infestation can be effectively simulated by making clusters of small holes with a nail or the point of a compass. Other signs of ageing, such as surface dents or chips along the edges of butt joints, can be made with a hammer and a craft knife respectively.

Left:
The restored pine cladding in the mud room of an 18th-century Rhode Island house reveals traces of the original paint.

3 Using a standard decorator's brush, roughly brush on a liberal quantity of antiquing glaze A over the entire surface.

Glaze

A Powder pigments: 1 part raw sienna, 1 part raw umber. Medium: 7 parts water, 3 parts PVA white glue. Ratios in glaze: 1 part pigment, 15 parts medium.

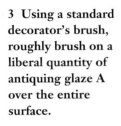

A

3

6

Ageing pine

4

5

4 Make a flat pad of a clean, lint-free cotton rag and rub the glaze into the grain and the small holes and scratches in the wood, at the same time as removing excess glaze from the surface. Keep turning the rag to form a clean pad as it becomes clogged with glaze.

Depending on room temperature, you have about an hour to complete this stage before the glaze dries. With something the size of a kitchen table top, the drying time won't be a problem. However, if you're ageing a large floor, you're advised to complete steps 2 and 3 on no more than two square yards or metres at a time – otherwise you won't be able to work all of glaze before it dries out.

The technique shown here for artificially ageing new pine can also be used to antique other pale or blonde woods, such as sycamore and birch. For darker woods, like mahogany, chestnut or walnut, you would need to increase the proportions of powder pigment in the antiquing glaze to achieve the desired effect.

5 Once the glaze has dried you have the option of repeating steps 3 and 4 if you wish to further darken the wood – although this hasn't been done in this example.

6 Surfaces likely to be exposed to moisture or excessive wear and tear – especially floors and table tops – should be protected with one or two coats of either matte, satin or gloss clear cellulose sealer.

85

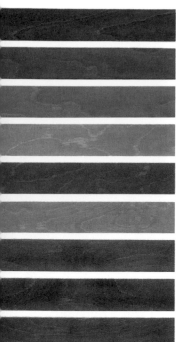

Left:
**A range of
traditional wood
stains shown after
varnishing (also
shown unvarnished
below). Note how
the varnish brings
out the depth of
colour.**

Overleaf:
**The Great Hall at
Parham House in
Sussex, England,
boasts the original
bleached oak
Elizabethan wall
panelling and door
casements.
Originally, panelling
was limed as a
deterrent against
insect infestation.**

Right:
**Decorator
Francesca Cullen
used coloured waxes
to pull together an
eclectic collection of
period panelling in
our 19th-century
London house.**

Staining, waxing and liming

Left:
**These test strips
show the effect of
different wood
stains on the same
piece of wood. Note
that the eventual
colour will be
affected by the base
colour of the wood
being stained.**

*I*n addition to using paints and glazes to
decorate joinery and furniture, painters and
decorators have traditionally also used various
stains and waxes and pastes containing lime to
embellish wooden surfaces. While most
paints are designed to provide an opaque
coloured finish that covers the underlying
wood, wood stains, waxes and liming pastes
allow the painter and decorator to either
change or enhance the natural colour of the
wood without obliterating its figuring or
grain. Consequently, it is almost always hardwoods which, unlike most softwoods, display
an almost infinite variety of attractive figuring
and graining, that are decorated in this manner – although some softwoods, such as various species of pine, can also be successfully
stained, waxed or limed.

Today, wood stains can be divided into four

main types: water-based stains; oil-based stains; spirit stains and chemical stains. Water-based stains, also known as direct dyes, are made by dissolving dry powder pigments with water and then making further dilutions until the required strength of colour has been achieved. The diluted pigments provide clear, vivid colours, they can be mixed together to produce a wide range of shades and they look particularly effective on light-coloured, close-grained woods, such as beech and pine. They do have, however, certain disadvantages over other types of stain. First, they tend to raise the grain of the underlying wood, which consequently needs to be smoothed down with fine-grade sandpaper after application. Second, they penetrate the surface of porous softwoods unevenly, which can result in patchy coloration. And third, they need to be sealed with either shellac or goldsize before they can be waxed and polished.

Oil-based wood stains are soluble in mineral spirits (white spirit) and are available pre-mixed in a variety of colours. Unlike water-based stains, they do not penetrate the fibres of the wood and thus do not raise the grain. They are also more transparent than water-based stains and provide more even coloration of the surface of the wood. However, the disadvantages of this type of stain are that they are relatively slow-drying and expensive.

Spirit-based wood stains are made by dissolving powder pigments in denatured alcohol (methylated spirits) and then adding French polish as a binder, in a ratio of four parts spirit to one part polish. Available in a variety of colours, they offer a duller finish than water-based stains, but they penetrate the wood quite deeply and therefore they provide an ideal base for French polishing. As such, spirit-based stains are most commonly used on oily or hard, fine-grained woods. However, they do have a tendency to lift the grain of the wood and, because of their rapid drying times, they are quite difficult to apply evenly over a large surface area.

Chemical wood stains are made by mixing chemicals such as ammonia, blue copperas, copper sulphate and bichromate of potash with water. They work by reacting with the tannic acid present in the wood and thus changing its natural colour. For example, bichromate of potash turns walnut a pale yellow colour and beech a light tan, while ammonia turns mahogany a deep brown with a grayish tone. Their one major disadvantage compared to other types of stain is that because of the difficulty in assessing the level of tannic acid present in wood, it is impossible to determine the resulting colour of the wood in advance of application.

Regular waxing and polishing of stained joinery and furniture with clear beeswax furniture polish helps to build up a protective lustrous sheen that enriches the natural colouring and enhances the appearance of the figuring and grain of the wood. Beeswax can also be tinted with burnt umber and black artist's oils and powder pigments (or be mixed with shoe polish), and used as an antiquing wax, particularly on period furniture. Some commercial beeswax polishes are available ready tinted to suit antique furniture in different woods.

In 16th-century Europe furniture and panelling made from open-grain woods like oak or ash was often treated with a caustic lime paste in order to lighten or "bleach" the wood and protect against insect infestation, as at Parham House (*see* previous page). The subtle effect produced by the white pigment left in the grain of the wood was much admired, and by the 17th century liming furniture and joinery had become a fashionable decorative effect. Today, proprietary liming pastes and waxes are available from specialist suppliers (*see* the Directory, pages 172-175). However, you can make up your own (*see* page 169) or produce a similar effect by rubbing white latex (emulsion) paint into the grain of wood (for technique, *see* overleaf).

Above:

A mistake has become a decorative effect: the woodstain reacted with a residue of chemical stripper in the wood to produce this ghostly blue-white hue, that is reminiscent of liming. To avoid this, make sure you neutralize the wood before staining. If you like the result, you can achieve a similar effect by using a latex/emulsion wash (*see* right).

Below:

Pale wood stains or an application of a liming paste (*see* p.169) will bleach pine floorboards to a whitish hue. The effect was originally produced by scrubbing with sand, as a method of clearing bare wood floors. It is particularly associated with Scandinavian-style period interiors.

For the liming technique shown here, white latex (matte emulsion) paint is used to produce the desired finish – an effective alternative to the traditional and more laborious method of liming with paste or wax made from animal glue. Shown on oak, liming can also be applied to pale woods such as pine, ash and elm.

1

2

1 Remove any layers of paint or varnish with a commercial stripper and allow the wood to dry thoroughly. Key the surface and open up the grain by rubbing over the wood (in the direction of the grain) with a wire brush. Then seal any knots with clear shellac (or knotting compound).

2 Using a standard decorator's brush, apply a coat of unthinned white latex (matte emulsion) paint. Over large areas, such as floors, work on no more than two square yards or metres at a time, or you won't have time to complete the next step before the paint dries.

3 Make up a flat pad from a clean, lint-free rag and rub the paint into the grain, at the same time as wiping off excess paint from the surface. Keep reforming the pad and changing the rag when necessary.

Limed oak

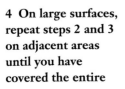

3

5

4 On large surfaces, repeat steps 2 and 3 on adjacent areas until you have covered the entire surface – taking care not to build up too great a density of paint where areas overlap.

5 Finally, allow the surface to dry overnight, and then brush on two coats of matte finish cellulose for protection. Allow approximately two hours drying time between coats.

Woodgraining

*F*or a proper appreciation of woodgraining as a decorative finish, it is necessary to recognize the crucial role that wood itself has played in the construction of man's environment. At the most basic level, wood has provided a source of heat and shelter and has often been essential for survival. Over and above this, wood has several inherent qualities that explain why it lies at the heart of primitive cultures and advanced civilizations alike. It is hard-wearing and inherently strong (many species perform well under both compression and tension) and can be cut and planed into a variety of shapes and thicknesses to produce housing, furniture, tools and other essential artefacts. Furthermore, it can be carved into aesthetically pleasing shapes and patterns, it has good insulating properties and is warm to the touch, and it can be stained, painted and varnished to enhance both its surroundings and its own longevity.

The physical properties of wood that have made it indispensable as a building material also explain its decorative appeal. The surface of sawn and planed timber reveals attractive graining and figuring (decorative markings) unique not only to each species and sub-species of tree, but also to different parts of a tree and to the way it has been cut (cutting wood horizontally or vertically produces quite distinct and different markings).

For our purposes, timber can be divided into two categories: hardwoods and softwoods. Most softwoods are fast-growing, have always been in plentiful supply in most parts of the world and, even today, are relatively inexpensive. But, being close-grained, and displaying little or no figuring beyond the odd randomly spaced knot, they are, with certain exceptions, rather bland in appearance.

Most hardwoods, on the other hand, can be cut to reveal intricate and highly decorative graining and figuring. Consequently, many species, such mahogany, walnut, oak, chestnut, bird's eye maple and rosewood, have always been highly sought-after for the construction of not only furniture, but also flooring, wall-panelling, doors, and many other architectural fixtures and mouldings. However, being slow-growing, the demand for hardwoods inevitably outstripped supply. And as their scarcity increased (in some cases as early as the 17th century), so they became increasingly expensive – especially those, such as mahogany and rosewood, imported to Europe from South America, Cuba and the Far East.

The initial response to the problems of scarcity and cost was an increasing use of veneers, particularly in the manufacture of furniture. For example, a chest-of-drawers that would once have been made of solid Cuban mahogany, would be constructed of a relatively inexpensive wood such as deal, then surfaced with a thin, mahogany veneer. Inevitably, high-quality veneers also increased in scarcity and price (beyond the pocket of many clients), so architects, builders and the makers of furniture turned to a less expensive solution: simulating the graining and figuring of wood with paints and glazes (woodgraining), just as they had turned to marbling (*see* pages 106-113) in the face of the lack of availability and prohibitive cost of marble.

The demand for woodgraining began in Europe during the early part of the 17th century. Initially confined to the homes of the wealthy, it was used to "convert" softwood wall-panelling, doors and dados into elaborately figured hardwoods, particularly in the "lesser" rooms or *salons*, in which the use of natural hardwoods was deemed to be both unnecessary and overly expensive.

By the middle of the 17th century woodgraining had gained recognition as a highly skilled technique and clients delighted in the expertise of their woodgrain painters, just as they did in the trompe l'oeil work (*see* pages 136-143) and the tortoiseshelling (*see* pages 128-129) also popular at the time. In each case the deception was considered an amusing display of superior knowledge. As it became increasingly fashionable, woodgraining found its way into some of the more important rooms and *salons*. A particularly fine example from the second half of the 17th century was the extravagant rosewood graining, in places over a gold leaf ground, on doors and dados in some of the rooms at Ham House in Surrey, England.

By the beginning of the 18th century, woodgraining had fallen out of fashion with wealthier home owners, who increasingly turned away from wall-panelling to the new hand-printed silks and wallpapers. However, with the increase in travel and trade in Europe, graining quietly gained in popularity among some of the more affluent sections of the middle classes. Between 1700 and 1750 a fully-panelled, hardwood-grained room was considered a solid symbol of material success. While some of the woodgraining of the 18th century was rather crudely done – particularly in less important homes – there was much that was subtly executed and bore a closer resemblance to the natural wood than many of the exuberant and somewhat theatrical illusions of the previous century had done.

In Europe an improvement in graining techniques, which resulted in ever-more-accurate facsimiles of various woods, was largely fuelled by an increasing dissemination of technical information on the subject. In

Above:
Gilded mouldings complement pale oak wood-graining.

Right:
By graining the radiator and the panelling the painter has minimized the presence of an obtrusive fitting.

Far right:
Bird's eye maple grained panelling.

Below:
A panelled window shutter, wood-grained in light oak.

1772 a Parisian, Watin, published a book on paint techniques called "*L'Art du Peinture, Doreur, Vernisseur*". Re-printed many times thereafter, it was one of the first of a number of similar books that contributed to an upsurge in demand for specialist decorating – particularly woodgraining and marbling – that lasted for much of the 19th century. Equally influential books on the subject included: "The Painter and Varnisher's Guide" (1804), the third edition of which (1830) contained a special section on woodgraining, and Nathaniel Whittock's "The Decorative Painter's and Glazier's Guide" (1827).

By 1836, the popularity of woodgraining in England had reached the point where John Loudon could write: "all woodwork . . . should be grained in imitation of some natural wood". A fine example of graining from this period is the oakgrained, pine-panelled hallway of Temple Newsam, in England, decorated in the Jacobean-revival style in 1830 (possibly by Wyatt).

However, while grained panelling remained a popular form of decoration in minor *salons*, hallways and withdrawing rooms in England up to approximately 1840, thereafter the introduction of mass-produced, and therefore more affordable, wallpapers saw a decline in the practice of panelling and woodgraining entire walls. Instead, painted graining was more often confined to woodwork – doors, skirtings or baseboards, stair, dado and picture rails or mouldings – and to built-in and free-standing furniture.

The leading exponent of woodgraining during the 19th century was Thomas Kershaw. Apprenticed in 1831 to John Platt of Bolton, Kershaw refined his skills in the north of England, before moving to London in 1843, where he began by working for building contractor, William Cubitt. Kershaw branched out on his own in 1850 and presented himself as "an expert grainer and marbler" at the London Great Exhibition of 1851, where his "imitation of foreign and English marbles and woods" won a first prize medal. Not content with existing equipment, he patented his own set of tools for graining in 1854.

An often controversial character, Kershaw caused a furore at the Paris Exhibition of 1855 where, after he had again won a first class medal, a French painter, stunned by the realistic appearance of his work, insisted that by some trickery Kershaw had used thin veneers of real wood instead of paints and glazes. Kershaw's response, an open demonstration of his graining techniques held at the shop of a French grainer, proved beyond any doubt that his work was genuine.

The publicity surrounding events at the Paris Exhibition did Kershaw's reputation and career nothing but good. In 1858 he was asked to work at Buckingham Palace in London, England, and he went on to work in many important London houses (before moving on to the provinces toward the end of his career). In 1860 Kershaw became a liveryman of the Paint-Stainer's Company. Within this group, painstaking effort was taken to deceive fellow grainers. The quality of the work produced was exceptional – the painted illusions often indiscernable from real wood, even under the closest scrutiny. (Fine examples survive at the Victoria and Albert Museum, in London.)

After approximately 1870 the demand for such specialist graining declined, although Kershaw believed that this was a temporary phase and was a consultant on Ellis A. Davidson's influential book "A Practical Manual of House-Painting, Graining, Marbing and Sign-Writing" (1874). Indeed, in the 1880s there was a resurgence of interest in graining that saw exotic woods such as bird's eye maple (*see* pages 104-5) used in drawing rooms and *salons*, and walnut and oak (*see* pages 102-3) in libraries, dining rooms and hallways. Chestnut, pine and maghogany (*see* pages 99-101) were also in demand.

For much of the 20th century, woodgraining has played a fairly minor role in interior decoration, and the work of Thomas Kershaw and his fellow 19th-century craftsmen remains the apogee of the art. However, it would be a mistake to believe that graining can only be considered successful if it is a painstakingly accurate copy of a real wood.

In North America and Scandinavia there has been a long tradition of "folk art graining" (in the case of the latter, dating back to the 17th century), in which itinerant craftsmen employed simple powder pigments and a variety of locally available mediums, such as beer, vinegar and even distemper, to grain panelling, wooden mouldings, furniture and other domestic artefacts. Using materials as diverse as cork, oil-card, leather, leaves and even their fingers to manipulate the glazes, they produced for their clients bold, exuberant and highly decorative sketches that in many cases bore only a faint resemblance to either the natural colour or the grain and figuring of any given wood. Such "fantasy" graining rarely deceives the onlooker into thinking he or she is looking at real wood, and in that sense has little in common with Kershaw's sophisticated facsimiles. However, like much of the extravagant graining executed in Europe in the late 17th century, it allows, with a knowing wink, the onlooker to participate in the joke that lies at the heart of the painted illusion, and is no less successful for that.

Left:
Fantasy woodgrained doors and panelling give a suitable period feel to the kitchen of Clifford Ellison's house, in England.

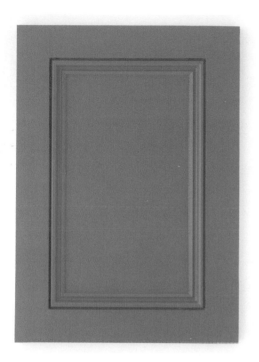

Left:
Inspired by rosewood, the flamboyant red and black "fantasy" graining on this door in Christophe Gollut's apartment accentuates the strident figuring characteristic of the natural wood. The adjacent architrave and skirting mouldings have been marbled.

Suitable for all manner of wooden surfaces, the mahogany graining technique illustrated here employs water-based glazes. These produce a crisper, more authentic-looking finish than oil-based glazes, but dry much faster than the latter. This means you must complete each stage, and move on to the next one, quite quickly. For this reason you are advised to thoroughly familiarize yourself with the grain, and practise the technique first on spare off-cuts of wood before you begin.

Paints and Glazes
A Rusty-brown eggshell paint.
B Powder pigments: 2 parts Van Dyke brown, 1 part raw umber, 1 part burnt umber. Medium: water. Ratios in glaze: 1 part pigments, 1 part medium.
C Powder pigments: 2 parts burnt umber, 1 part Van Dyke brown, 1 part raw umber. Medium: water. Ratios in glaze: 1 part pigments, 1 part medium.
D Powder pigments: 1 part Van Dyke brown, 1 part black. Medium: water. Ratios in glaze: 1 part pigments, 3 parts medium.

Mahogany graining

3

1 Using a standard decorator's brush, apply two coats of rusty-brown eggshell paint A onto the previously primed and undercoated door. You should allow each coat to dry for approximately 24 hours.

2 Wipe a thin coat of ground chalk (whiting) over the surface with a clean damp cloth.

3 Mix up mid-brown glaze B and, using a 2in (5cm) decorator's brush, roughly brush it out over the middle panel and mouldings. Then drag a small spalter (mottler) through the glaze on the panel in a series of slightly overlapping vertical sweeps.

4 To create heart grain on the panel, drag the small spalter (mottler) through the wet glaze in a series of overlapping elongated arcs. Start at the bottom of the panel and work upward. Each arc should be completed in a continuous sweep – don't pause at the apex of a curve.

Subtle streaks of darker graining can be introduced by occasionally dipping the bristles of the spalter (mottler) into glaze C. The heart graining will look more authentic if it is offset slightly to one side of the middle panel.

5 Soften and blend the graining using a badger softener. Start at the bottom centre of the heart grain, and lightly brush over the glaze in a series of short upward and outward sweeps (to the left and right), working your way up to the top of the panel. Wipe off any build-up of glaze on the bristles with rag.

6 Using a 1in (2.5 cm) artist's brush, apply a little more of glazes B and C to the mouldings around the middle panel. Working on one section of moulding at a time – horizontals first, verticals second – drag the brush through the glaze in a continuous sweep from one mitred corner to the other.

7 Having applied glaze B to the top and bottom sections of the frame, drag the small spalter (mottler) square-on through the glaze in one continuous horizontal sweep. Again, darker streaks can be introduced by dipping into glaze C. Then, straight away soften and blend the grain in the same direction with the badger softener, and keep cleaning the bristles with a lint-free damp rag.

8 Repeat step 7 on the upright sections, but this time drag the spalter (mottler) at an angle through the glaze to accentuate the bands of graining.

9 Allow the glaze to dry for four hours, then apply one coat of clear gloss polyurethane varnish. Leave this to dry for 24 hours.

10 Having applied another coat of ground chalk (whiting), brush glaze D onto the middle panel and moulding with the decorator's brush. Then drag the spalter (mottler) vertically through the glaze as you did in step 3.

100

9

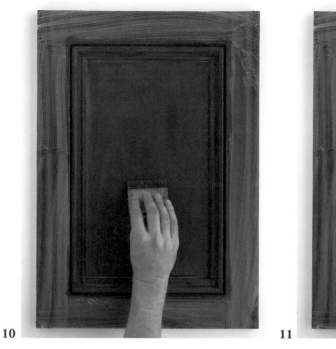

10

11

12

11 Lightly gripping a long-handled flogger parallel to the surface, employ a loose, wristy action to tap the bristles up and down the panel and moulding. Keep cleaning the bristles on a damp rag.

Then repeat steps 10 and 11 on the frame – horizontals first, verticals second – tapping in the direction of the grain.

12 The flogger removes small flecks of glaze to create the small pores characteristic of the grain.

13 Allow to dry for four hours, then apply one coat of satin or gloss clear polyurethane varnish.

1 *2* *3*

A

B

C

D

E

Oak graining

Paints and Glazes

A Bamboo coloured eggshell paint.

B Artist's oils: 7 parts raw sienna, 3 parts raw umber. Medium: 3 parts transparent oil glaze, 2 parts mineral spirits (white spirit). Ratios in glaze: 1 part pigments, 12 parts medium.

C Artist's oils: 2 parts raw sienna, 1 part raw umber. Medium: 4 parts transparent oil glaze, 5 parts mineral spirits (white spirit). Ratios in glaze: 1 part pigment, 8 parts medium.

D Artist's oils: 2 parts raw sienna, 1 part raw umber. Medium: 3 parts transparent oil glaze, 2 parts mineral spirits (white spirit). Ratios in glaze: 1 part pigments, 7 parts medium.

E Artist's oils: 3 parts burnt umber, 1 part black. Medium: 3 parts transparent oil glaze, 2 parts mineral spirits (white spirit). Ratios in glaze: 1 part pigments, 40 parts medium.

1 Having applied two coats of paint A to the previously primed and undercoated door, and allowed each coat to dry overnight, roughly brush out pale brown glaze B over the middle panel and frame.

2 Again using a 2in (5cm) standard decorator's brush, drag the bristles through the glaze in a series of slightly overlapping parallel sweeps to establish the direction of the grain. Complete the middle panel first – vertically; then the top and bottom of the frame – horizontally; and finally, the left and right sides – again vertically.

At the end of each sweep, wipe the bristles on a clean lint-free rag dampened with mineral spirits (white spirit) to remove the build-up of glaze.

3 Grain and texture the middle panel by lightly gripping a small badger softener and, using a loose wristy action, tapping (flogging) the sides of the bristles up and down the surface in a series of slightly overlapping, vertical parallel bands. (It is a good idea to practise this technique first on a spare off-cut of wood.)

As in step 3, keep cleaning the bristles on a rag dampened with mineral spirits (white spirit) to remove the build-up of glaze.

Next, repeat the technique on the top and bottom of the frame, and then on the sides – always in the direction of the grain.

The flogging action removes flecks of glaze from the surface to create the small irregular-shaped pores characteristic of the oak grain.

When you've finished, leave the surface to dry for approximately 24 hours.

4 Having applied a thin coat of transparent oil glaze over the middle panel with a clean cotton rag, and allowed it to become tacky (this

should take about 15 minutes), start to paint in the heart grain using glaze C and a ½in (1cm) flat fitch. Begin just off-centre and work outward, using the illustration for guidance as to composition. (*Note:* Practise this technique first on a spare off-cut of wood.)

5 When you've completed about a third of the panel, lightly flick the bristles of a small badger softener over the wet glaze. Work from out to in – in other words, always toward the enclosed heart of the grain.

102

4

5

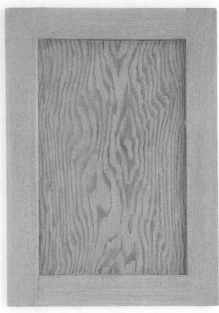

6

7

8

6 Repeat steps 6-7 until you've completed the heart graining, and then lightly flog the panel with a small badger softener and the technique used in step 4.

7 Having applied glaze D to the four sides of the frame, drag the brush used in step 3 at a slight angle through the glaze to accentuate the darker and lighter bands of graining. As before, complete the top and bottom rails first, before doing the sides – always dragging in the direction of the grain.

Then, lightly flog the four sides with a badger softener, again as you did in step 4.

8 Leave the door to dry for 24 hours, and then give it a coat of matte or satin finish clear polyurethane varnish for protection.

9 Alternatively, if you wish to artificially age the door, brush on a coat of antiquing glaze E, building up a thicker layer in the recesses around the middle panel, and allow it to dry before applying the varnish.

For additional information on antiquing wood-grained surfaces – including a simple spattering technique for the simulation of woodworm and beetle infestation – see Antiquing, on page 73.

9

1 Using a 2in (5cm) standard decorator's brush, apply two coats of paint A to the primed and undercoated box. Allow each coat to dry for 12 hours.

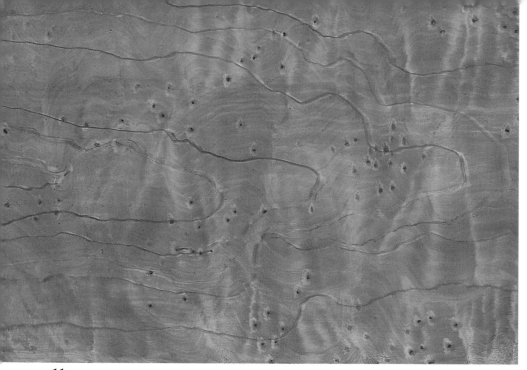

11

Bird's eye maple graining

A

B

C

2

3

Paints and Glazes

A 4 parts pale yellow eggshell, 1 part raw umber artist's oil.
B Powder pigments: 2 parts raw umber, 3 parts raw sienna. Medium: 1 part vinegar (acetic acid), 9 parts water. Ratios in glaze: 1 part pigments, 1 part medium.
C 1 part burnt sienna, 1 part burnt umber.

Medium: 1 part vinegar, 9 parts water. Ratios in glaze: 1 part pigments, 3 parts medium.

As with the mahogany graining on pages 99-101, the bird's eye maple graining technique illustrated here employs water- rather than oil-based glazes in order to produce a crisper, more authentic-looking finish. Because of the fast drying times, you will have to complete each step, and move on to the next one, quite quickly. Consequently you are once again advised to familiarize yourself with the grain and practise the technique on spare off-cuts of wood before starting in earnest.

2 Wipe a thin coat of white chalk (whiting) over the lid with a damp rag.

3 Brush on glaze B, and finish off with a series of vertical parallel strokes.

4 Drag a small spalter (mottler) down through the glaze in a series of overlapping bands. Introduce a random undulating movement to the left and right during each drag, in order to leave darker concentrations of glaze at various points on the surface and establish the basic pattern of the grain. At the end of each drag, clean the bristles with a damp rag.

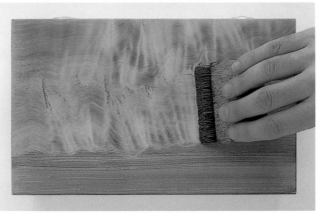

4

8

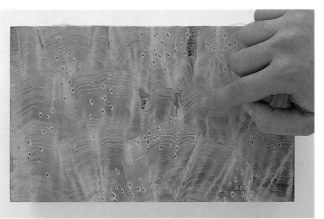

5

9

6

10

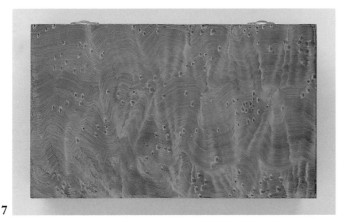

7

5 Wet the tip of a forefinger in a solution consisting of 1 part vinegar (acetic acid) and 9 parts water, and lightly dab it in random clusters over the surface. The vinegar solution will cause a localized cissing action in the glaze and create the oval-shaped bird's eyes that are character-istic of the grain.

6 Soften the outlines of the graining and bird's eyes by gently stroking the bristles of a badger softener in all directions over the surface. Again, clean the bristles with a damp rag at regular invervals. Then repeat steps 2-6 on the sides and bottom of the box, and allow to dry for four hours.

7 Using a varnishing brush, apply one coat of gloss or satin finish clear polyurethane varnish to, in turn, the top, sides and bottom of the box. Again leave the varnish to dry for 24 hours.

8 Having wiped another coat of ground chalk onto the lid, brush on glaze C and drag the spalter (mottler) down through it in a series of slightly overlapping parallel bands. You should clean the bristles with a damp rag after each drag.

9 Mix small and equal quantities of the pigments used in glaze C and dilute them 3 parts pigments to 1 part water. Then, using a small artist's brush, touch in the darker middles of the bird's eyes and the thin wavy bands of darker grain.

10 Repeat steps 8-9 on the sides and bottom of the box, allowing each to dry for four hours.

11 Finally, apply one coat of satin or gloss finish clear polyurethane varnish to all sides of the box, and allow to dry for 24 hours.

Marbling

Right:
Faux marble panelling in a bathroom of the Chateau d'O, in Orme, France. The strident diagonal accents of the veining contrasts sharply with the pale pastel background colours and contributes to the sense of solidity in the finish.

Right:
Various fantasy *faux* marble and stone finishes and finely executed trompe l'oeil work are boldy combined in a *salon* of the Chateau d'O at Orme. The radiator has been "disguised" by giving it the same *faux* stone finish as the trompe l'oeil dado panel behind.

Marble ("shining stone", from the Greek) is defined as "any rock whose surface is capable of taking a decorative polish". The finest examples – characterized by deposits of colourful minerals (such as quartz, opal, and turquoise) that appear on or just below the surface, usually in the form of an intricate system of veins – lend an air of solidity, formality and opulence to their surroundings. Not surprisingly, marble has been one of the most prestigious of building materials since Classical Greek and Roman times.

Decorative painters were employed to simulate marble with paint (marbling) for two main reasons. First, the cost of quarrying, cutting and polishing marble made it expensive, and transportation costs from the quarries, mainly in Italy (notably Carrara) and France, were high. Second, because most marbles, being dense, performed well under compression but poorly under tension, they could be used in block form to construct columns and walls, as slabs for flooring and as thin veneers for cladding, but were unsuitable for ceilings, overhangs or beams. Consequently, even when cost was not a factor, marble was often used in combination with the painted illusion.

Sophisticated marbling began on a large scale during the Renaissance in Italy and France. The fine examples that adorned many important civic and residential buildings established a tradition of precise, formal and flamboyant marbling that has survived in both countries up to this day.

In 17th-century England, the sumptuous interiors of many palaces and large houses – reflecting the Italian influence – featured imaginative, if somewhat crudely executed marbled panelling, plasterwork, columns and joinery. Although it was less fashionable for much of the 18th century (in part due to the influx of Italian craftsmen working in *scagliola*, marbling enjoyed an upsurge of popular demand throughout the 19th century, when it was not unusual to find entire rooms decorated in *faux marbre*. The greatest exponents of the art during this period, Thomas Kershaw and John Taylor, produced facsimiles that maintained the illusion even under the closest scrutiny. (Specimens of their work, notably yellow sienna, serpentine, rouge royal and red levanto, survive at the Victoria and Albert museum in London, and the Chadwick museum in Bolton.)

Many fine examples, indistinguishable from the real stone, can also be found throughout Scandinavia. However, since the 18th century, Scandinavia has also had a strong regional tradition of naive ("farmer") marbling, in which crude marble effects run riot over every available surface. Such stylized "fantasy" marbling (echoed in the gaudy colours and opaque patterning of much North American marbling) may not display the accurate configurations, subtle translucency and depths of colour found in Kershaw and Taylor's replications, but is technically more accessible and has a charming spontaneity that suggests rather than states the illusion.

ERATO

Right:
The classical proportions of the octagonal study in Richard Jenrette's house on the Hudson River, in North America, are accentuated by marbled-block walls, contrasting marbled skirtings (baseboards) and marble pedestals.

Top left:
Contrasting fantasy *faux marbre* and *faux* stone wall panelling at the Chateau d'O in Orme in France.

Middle left:
Yellow sienna *faux* marble wall panelling and contrasting black and gold *faux* marble skirting (baseboard) on the hallway staircase at the Sir John Soane Museum in London, England.

Bottom left:
Heavily veined, fantasy sienna-marbled wall panels at the Chateau d'O in Orme, France.

Paints and Glazes

A Dark bamboo eggshell paint.
B Black eggshell paint.
C Artist's oils: 4 parts yellow ochre, 3 parts white, 2 parts burnt sienna.
Medium: 2 parts transparent oil glaze, 1 part mineral spirits (white spirit). Ratios in glaze: 1 part pigments, 15 parts medium.
D Artist's oils: 10 parts white, 2 parts yellow ochre, 1 part burnt sienna.
Medium: as in glaze C above.
Ratios in glaze: 1 part pigments, 10 parts medium.
E Artist's oils: 1 part yellow ochre, 1 part burnt sienna, 1 part white.
Medium: as C above.
Ratios in glaze: as C above.

1 Apply two coats of black paint **B** to the previously primed and undercoated base/skirting board. Allow to dry for 24 hours after each coat.

Note: In this example the wall above was decorated with two coats of eggshell paint **A**.

2 Having masked off the wall and floor with tape, apply a thin coat of transparent oil glaze over the skirting with a rag. Then, using a ¾in (1.5cm) flat fitch, and dipping the bristles alternately into glazes **C**, **D** and **E**, loosely brush on the basic shapes of the veining chains. Work on one chain at a time. As you can see in the illustration, the colours of each chain subtly change along their lengths – hence the use of three glazes.

3 Soften and blend each chain immediately after you've completed it, by lightly brushing the wet glazes with the bristle tips of a small badger softener.

In addition to following the black and gold marbling illustrations shown here, you should, if possible, take a close look at the natural stone itself. By doing this you will learn a great deal about its subtle structure – notably the loosely linked, chain-like formation of veins that lie on or just below the surface. As always, practise on spare off-cuts of wood, before you begin.

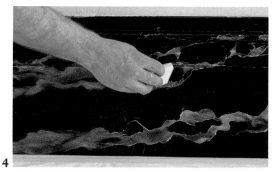

1

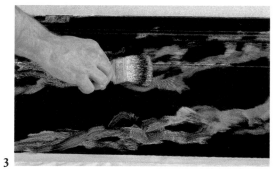

2

3

Black and gold marble

4 Pull the hard edge of a plastic eraser through the wet glaze to cut out and reinforce the basic shape of the veins. Although this looks complicated, by copying the illustration and practising the technique on an off-cut of wood you will soon learn how to move the glaze over the surface, coalescing it into thin, hard edges, and thus defining the irregular-shaped links that make up the major chains.

Note: As you work, keep wiping off the build-up of glaze on the eraser onto a clean rag.

5 Using a small, square-bristled artist's brush, and again dipping into glazes **C**, **D** and **E**, apply the thin filaments that either shoot out of, or in some cases link, sections of the main veining chains. As you can see, the shape of these filaments varies. However, they all broadly follow the predominantly diagonal accent of the main veins.

6 Repeat the technique with the hard-edged eraser shown in step 4 to extend and further define the shape of the thin filaments introduced in the last step.

7 Use the tip of a cotton swab to carefully remove any spots of glaze left in and between the main veins.

4

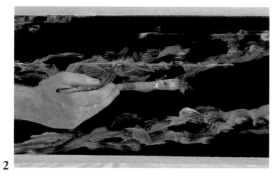

5

8 Lightly soften and blend the filaments and veins using a badger softener, as in step 3. Allow to dry for 24 hours.

9 Mix a pale white glaze from 1 part white artist's oil to 10 parts of a medium of equal quantities of transparent oil glaze and mineral spirits (white spirit). Wipe a thin coat of transparent oil glaze over the surface with a rag, then apply the white glaze with a small artist's brush to form the secondary (ghost) veins that link the major veins and filaments. Soften and blend each vein with a badger softener immediately after brushing it on.

12

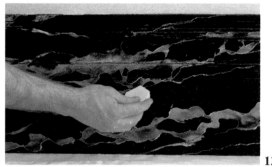

6

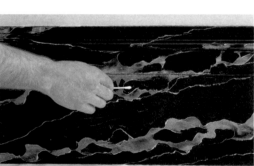

7

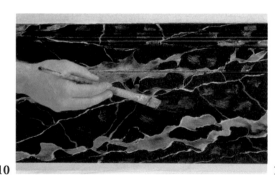

10

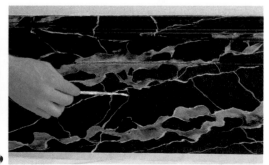

11

10 Mix up another translucent white glaze, this time consisting of 1 part white artist's oil to approximately 35 parts of a medium again consisting of equal quantities of transparent oil glaze and mineral spirits (white spirit).

Then, using a ¾in inch (1.5cm) artist's brush, apply the glaze to form the oval-shaped fossil forms that lie just below the surface and in and between the main veining chains. Again, soften and blend each group of fossil forms with a badger softening brush immediately after you've brushed them on.

11 Allow the surface to dry thoroughly for approximately 24 hours, then carefully remove the masking tape from the top and bottom of the skirting.

12 Finally, apply one or two coats of satin or gloss clear polyurethane varnish for added protection, and allow 24 hours drying time after each coat.

For a more lustrous finish, the surface can be rubbed down with fine-grade wet-and-dry paper prior to polishing with furniture wax.

111

Arabescato fiorenzo marble

As with black and gold marbling on pages 110-11, you will find it a great help when simulating Arabescato Fiorenzo to examine a piece of the natural stone in addition to following the step-by-step illustrations shown here.

1 Having primed and undercoated the surface of the column, apply two coats of white eggshell paint and allow 24 hours drying time after each one.

2 Using a 2in (5cm) standard decorator's brush, stipple on glaze A to form the basic shapes of the primary veining system. To some extent the pattern you establish is a matter of personal composition. However, use the illustration for guidance and note that the areas of the column where you apply the least glaze will be the sites of the secondary veins.

3 Use the bristle tips of a ¾in (2cm) flat-bristled artist's brush to push and coalesce the glaze into the irregular-shaped links of the primary veining chains.

1

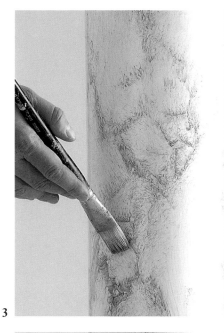

2

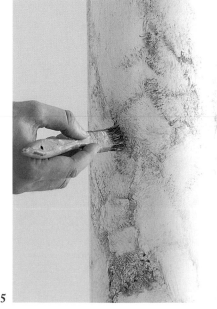

3

4 Employ the same technique and a 1½in (4cm) standard decorator's brush to create the fainter secondary veins.

5 Dipping the bristles of a 1in (2.5cm) standard decorator's brush alternately into pale green and pale yellow glazes B and C, stipple on translucent patches of broken colour around the edges of the primary veins.

4

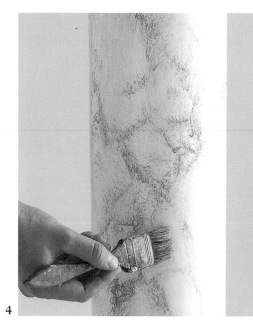

5

6

7

6 Gently stipple over the wet glazes with a large, soft-bristled jamb duster brush to get rid of any obtrusive brush marks on the surface.

7 Lightly flick the bristle tips of a badger softener over the wet glazes to soften and blend the primary and secondary veins. Then allow to dry for 24 hours.

8 Having wiped on a thin coat of transparent oil glaze with a clean rag, use a small, flat-bristled artist's brush and glaze D to create the irregular-shaped mineral deposits characteristic of the marble.

Note: While most of the deposits lie along, or follow, the paths of the primary veins, a few are isolated on the secondary veins.

9 Gently soften and blend the glazes with a badger softener immediately after you've brushed them on. Leave to dry for 24 hours.

10 Having repeated steps 2-9 on the cap and base of the column, and allowed the glazes to dry, apply one or two coats of satin or gloss clear polyurethane varnish. Finally, for a more lustrous finish, polish with furniture wax.

Paints and Glazes

A Artist's oils: 3 parts raw umber, 3 parts black, 2 parts veridian. Medium: 3 parts transparent oil glaze, 2 parts mineral spirits (white spirit). Ratios in glaze: 1 part pigments, 30 parts medium.

B As glaze A above, but add ¼ part raw sienna artist's oil.

C As glaze A above, but add ¼ part more veridian and add ¼ part more black artist's oils.

D Artist's oils: 2 parts raw umber, 2 parts black, 1 part veridian. Medium: 2 parts transparent oil glaze, 1 part mineral spirits (white spirit). Ratios in glaze: 1 parts pigments, 7 parts medium.

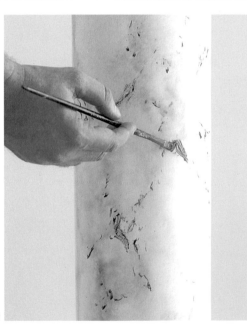

8

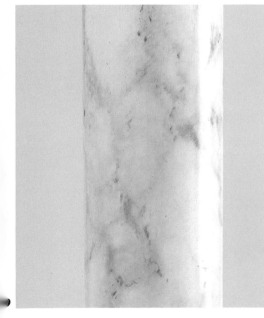

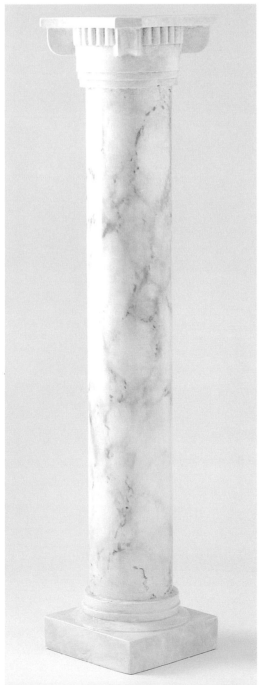

10

Stonework

*I*n addition to the often intricately veined pure marbles quarried, cut and polished from metamorphic rock (*see* pages 106-113), and the elaborately patterned decorative stones, such as breccias, travertines and fossiliverous and variegated limestones, extracted from sedimentary rock, architects have also employed more uniformly patterned stones, such as porphyry, sandstone and granite, in the construction and decoration of buildings. Cut from igneous rock, they display few structural imperfections and are often unpolished. And like marble, when the natural stone has been either unavailable, prohibitively expensive or structurally unsuitable (*see* page 106), decorative painters have been called upon to simulate it in paint.

For example, porphyry (from the Greek *porphyrite*, meaning purple) is a granular rock found in many parts of the world and often used, like granite, as a facing stone or for architrave, furniture (desk and table tops) and other artefacts (plinths). While the English stone tends to be a reddish-orange colour, the French is predominantly green and violet and the Scandinavian flecked with pink, red and green, and sometimes veined with quartz. *Faux* porphyry is created by spattering appropriately coloured glazes over an opaque basecoat and gradually building up the flecks of colour characteristic of the natural stone. (For spattering technique *see* Antiquing, pages 72-73.) Porphyry imitations can be seen in, for example, Egyptian murals, on the walls of Pompeii, in

Italian and French buildings dating from the Renaissance to the present day, and in many classically inspired 18th- and 19th-century English and North American interiors.

Historically, stone-blocking has been one of the most popular of *faux* stone effects. Stones that perform well under compression, such as sandstone and granite were, like marble, often used either in block form for the construction of walls, or as slabs for flooring and cladding. To simulate this, broken colour techniques (*see* pages 56-67) such as spattering and sponging were employed to build up the colour and coarse or smooth texture of individual blocks and slabs, while a simpe trompe l'oeil effect accounted for the mortar joints and gave the surface a three-dimensional appearance.

Finely detailed and highly convincing examples of stone-blocking can be found in classically inspired Italian and French interiors from the Renaissance onward; in aristocratic and upper-middle class English homes, particularly at the end of the 18th and the beginning of the 19th centuries, and in the entrances, stairwells and reception rooms of North American Empire-style houses. However, with stone-blocking, as with marbling and woodgraining, the suggestion of the illusion can be as effective as a painstakingly accurate replication – witness the fashion in Medieval times of simply marking out white plastered walls with red lines to imitate masonry.

1

1 Having applied two coats of paint A to the previously undercoated surface, and allowed each coat to dry overnight, carefully mark the outlines of the stone blocks using a spirit-level, a straight edge and a pencil.

2 Using 5mm low-tack masking tape, mask off each block from those surrounding it. Position the tape on the side of each line furthest from the predominant light source (here, off top left) – in other words, below all horizontals and to the right of all verticals. This will ensure that when the tape is removed the 'shadows' cast by the groutlines will be on the correct side, and that the flat surface takes on a three-dimensional look.

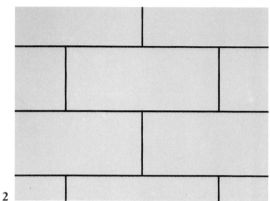

2

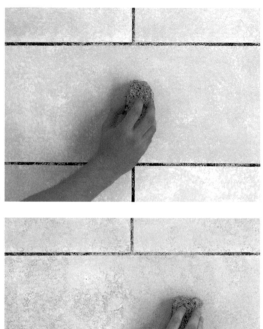

3 Using a small marine or textured decorator's sponge, and working on a maximum of five blocks at a time, gently dab on glaze B in overlapping, irregular-shaped patches of broken colour. Don't obliterate the base colour and avoid creating any obvious pattern across the surface.

4 Before glaze B dries, repeat step 3 with glaze C and a new sponge – only this time the patches of colour should be fewer and further between, and should vary from block to block.

5 Again, before glazes B and C have dried, repeat step 4 with glaze D and another new sponge. As before, for an authentic finish vary the application of colour so that the blocks don't appear identical.

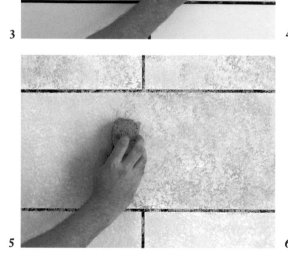

5

6 Working on one block at a time, and using the sponge used in step 3, lightly dab over the wet surface to soften and blend the three glazes into a lightly textured, speckled finish. Again, try to work the glazes so that no one block looks the same as another.

7 Having repeated steps 3-6 on the rest of the wall (five blocks at a time), and allowed the surface to dry for 24 hours, carefully peel off the masking tape. Then rub out the pencil marks at the points where they overlap the groutlines between the blocks.

4

7

8 Finally, apply a coat of clear matte polyurethane or water-based varnish for protection.

Paints and Glazes

A Ivory eggshell paint.

B Artist's oil: raw sienna. Medium: 1 part transparent oil glaze, 1 part white oil-based undercoat. Ratios in glaze: 1 part pigment, 10 parts medium.

C Artist's oils: 2 parts raw sienna, 1 part Payne's gray. Medium: as B above. Ratios in glaze: 1 parts pigments, 15 parts medium.

D Artist's oils: 1 part Payne's gray, 1 part raw umber. Medium: as B above. Ratios in glaze: 1 part pigments, 12 parts medium.

Stone blocking

9 This example was created using broadly the same technique as in steps 1-8. However, instead of using masking tape (step 2 was dropped) the grout lines between blocks were defined by dragging a hard-edged rubber at an angle through the glaze (new step 7: for technique *see* black and gold marbling, pages 110-11). The paints and glazes used were:

A White eggshell oil paint.

B Artist's oil: Paynes gray. Medium: 3 parts transparent oil glaze, 2 parts mineral spirits (white spirit). Ratios in glaze: 1 part pigment, 20 parts medium.

C Artist's oils: 2 parts Indian red, 1 part veridian. Medium and ratios in glaze: as B above.

D Artist's oils: 2 parts Payne's gray, 1 part raw umber, 1 part raw sienna. Medium and ratios in glaze: as B above.

9

8

119

Ornamental finishes

*T*hroughout history, precious materials such as gold and tortoiseshell have been used to embellish a variety of surfaces in grand interiors. Until the discovery of platinum in the 18th century, gold was the most precious and valuable of metals and the art of gilding developed as an ingenious method of spreading a very thin layer of gold, either in leaf or powder form, over a less costly surface such as plaster or wood.

There are three main methods of gilding: oil gilding, water gilding and powder gilding. Oil gilding involves placing thin sheets of gold leaf (nowadays supplied in booklet form on sheets of waxed tissue paper, and also available in silver and a variety of other metals), over goldsize (an oil-based varnish) while the size is still tacky. The size can be painted directly onto wood, sealed plaster or, traditionally, a gesso ground. *Gesso* gives the gilding a silky smooth finish and makes it colder to the touch than wooden or plaster grounds. Although usually white, *gesso* can also be coloured (traditionally red). The intention is that the colour ghosts through the gilding, or is revealed in tiny cracks in the surface, and thus gives the finish a warm glow.

Water gilding is a highly skilled process that takes an apprentice gilder several years to master. It involves floating thin sheets of gold over coloured clay (known as bole). The gilding takes on a different hue, depending on the underlying colour (red and blue are traditional) and has a particularly lustrous finish, especially after it has been burnished. Examples of water gilding dating back more than 3000 years have been found in the tombs of the Egyptian pharoahs, and include the mask of Tutankhamen's mummy.

Powder gilding is mainly used by professionals for touching up awkward areas, such as highly intricate plaster mouldings, where the gold or silver leaf would not stick to the surface. The technique involves sprinkling metallic powders over a surface coated with goldsize, shaking off excess powder and then

Right and far right:
Gilded chairs and wooden and plaster mouldings in the Grand *Salon* of the Chateau de Compiegne in France. The room was originally decorated for the Empress Josephine by the painters Redoute and Dubois. The decorative finishes were restored extensively during the 1950s.

Right:
In 1912 the Edwardian library at Temple Newsam, in England, was "converted" by Lenygons of London into a replica of an elegant early Georgian library. The room boasts flat-painted, sage-green walls and contrasting ornate gilded plaster mouldings, mirrors and picture frames.

burnishing to produce a lustrous finish. While the amateur gilder will find metallic powders an effective substitute for transfer metal leaf, they should never be used to restore valuable antique gilded furniture.

In Britain, gilding has been used to decorate the homes of the wealthy since Stuart times, particularly as a method of embellishing carved woodwork. Gilding also featured strongly in Baroque and Rococo interiors, especially in continental Europe. The style reached its apogee at the Palace of Versailles, in France, where the onlooker was dazzled with a glittering array of gilt mirrors reflecting an abundance of heavily gilded artefacts and furniture. English taste, however, was rather more reserved, and gilt furniture was considered ostentatious until the end of the 17th century.

In the first quarter of the 18th century, gilding played an important role in classically inspired interiors. The flutes of columns would be emphasized with gilding of various hues (depending on the colour of the underlying bole or *gesso*), and a particularly ornate wooden or plaster moulding could be picked out with as many as three different tones. The English architect William Kent, for example, used gilding on coffered ceilings and staircases and in the drawing rooms and ballrooms he designed which were based on the white and gold schemes of the classical Italian architect Andrea Palladio.

The 18th-century European vogue for Chinoiserie also involved gilding. For example, Chinese-style mirror frames were gilded and gilt filets were used to frame hand-painted Chinese wallpaper panels, and objects such as trays and tea caddies made of tin (*tole* ware) were gilded to resemble Oriental lacquerwork.

However, for most of the 18th century it was France, rather than the Orient, that provided architects, designers and decorators with inspiration in the use of gilding. French influence can be seen in many of the ornate interiors at Southill Park in England, and spread as far as Scandinavia, where Swedish painters decorated the mouldings outlining white or blue-gray panels in gold leaf, and gilded chairs in the French style.

During the 19th century, gilding continued to be used as a show of opulence and the expanding merchant classes of Europe invested in heavy gilt picture frames which complemented rich polycromatic wall and ceiling schemes decorated with elaborate plasterwork, often picked out in gilt. The late 19th-century artistic backlash to the vulgarity of the High Victorian taste still featured gilding; this time set against stained black woodwork in an aesthetic interpretation of an oriental theme.

The Neo-classical revival at the start of the 20th century saw a return to white and gilt rooms, while elaborate gilded pieces such as shell chairs re-emerged with the 1920s fashion for the neo-Baroque style. (Gilded chinoiserie furniture in the 18th-century style was also reproduced during this period.) The 1920s and 1930s also heralded the Art Deco movement and a fresh approach to metallic wall finishes, with gold or silver leaf being applied in squares, or metallic paint being spattered over a plain ground.

Although gold was more commonly used than silver before the 20th century, silver-gilt was known to have been used as early as the late 1660s, when a room in Rosenberg Castle, Copenhagen, Denmark, was decorated in silver-gilt and *faux* tortoiseshell.

Tortoiseshell, a semi-translucent, mottled material from the shell of the hawksbill turtle, was first used as an ornamental veneer in the East and is thought to have been brought to Europe by merchants of the East India Company. A brown and yellow coloration was the most common, but red and black was also found. A late 17th-century treatise mentions the popularity of *faux* tortoiseshell for decorating cabinets and tables, and together with woodgraining (*see* pages 93-105) and trompe l'oeil (*see* pages 136-143), tortoiseshelling became the height of fashion among the *cognoscenti* of the period.

During the 18th century real tortoiseshell inlay was used on furniture, notably by the Frenchman André Boulle, cabinetmaker to Louis XIV. Lesser makers, however, resorted to the skills of the painter to overcome a shortage of the natural material.

The decoration of wooden furniture with an imitation tortoiseshell paint effect was also common in country districts of North America, where a streaky black and red finish was especially popular.

Right:

Antiqued gilded wood and plaster mouldings, heavily stained and waxed wood and a preponderance of rich reds and deep blues throughout the room are quintessentially 19th-century Victorian-Gothic.

Overleaf:

A sumptuous combination of gilded furniture and decorative mouldings, *faux marbre* walls and silk fabrics in The *Grand Salon*, a formal First Empire room at the Chateau de Compiegne, in France.

Gilding

Applying gold leaf

1 Having rubbed down painted surfaces with 0 grade steel (wire) wool, removed grease or dust with a lint-free rag and white (mineral) spirits, and sealed bare wood or plaster with a suitable primer, brush on a coat of gold size.

2 When the gold size feels tacky (it should take a fingerprint), place a sheet of gold leaf on top of the moulding. Rub over the wax paper backing sheet with either a finger or a stiff hog's hair brush. Apply a firm and consistent pressure all over the sheet.

3 Carefully remove the wax paper, leaving the gold leaf stuck on the moulding. Each subsequent strip of leaf should overlap the previous one. However, it is not essential to fill every crevice as irregularities in the finish will add to the antique effect.

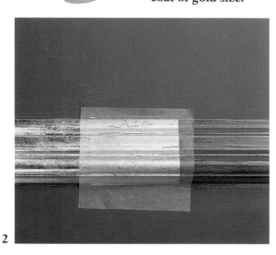

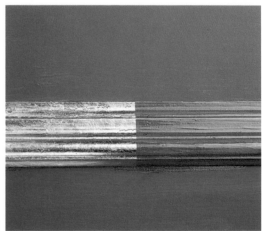

4 Use an artist's brush to sweep away metal debris from the newly gilded surface. (If you accidently damage the gold leaf simply rub on a small repair patch.) Then moisten a clean rag with mineral spirits, and carefully rub away any excess gold leaf round the edges of the moulding. Leave for between three to four hours, by which time the gold size will have dried.

5 Rub down the gilding with fine grade 000 steel (wire) wool, concentrating on raised areas most exposed to wear and tear.

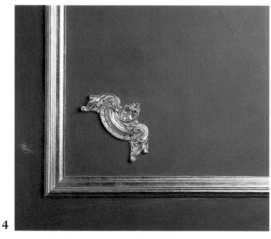

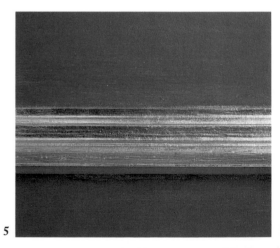

6 Brush on a coat of either tinted furniture wax or clear oil-based varnish thinned with mineral spirits and tinted with a small quantity of burnt umber artist's oil.

7 Once the surface has dried (roughly 24 hours if varnish has been used), rub it down with fine grade 000 steel (wire) wool. Then apply a second coat of wax or tinted varnish, and when this has dried finish off by waxing and polishing.

1

Applying bronze powder

1 Using a small decorator's brush, apply a coat of tinted gold size to the surface of the moulding. Make sure you don't miss any patches, or the metallic powder won't adhere to the surface and will simply drop off.

2 When the gold size becomes tacky, use a hog's hair brush to stipple bronze powder onto the moulding. When you have finished, lightly dust with a large squirrelhead mop to remove any loose powder. Then allow the underlying size to dry for 36 hours.

2

3

4

3 Next, use a clean, lint-free rag to gently rub down the gilding. You can expect a fair amount of powder to come off onto the rag. By rubbing harder – don't overdo it – some of the ground colour will ghost through, helping to create a pleasantly worn look.

4 To simulate further ageing, gently rub down the surface with fine grade 000 steel (wire) wool, concentrating on the raised areas and edges most exposed to natural wear and tear.

5

5 Use a tinted wax to darken down the colour of the bronze powder, applying it with a small artist's brush. Make sure you don't accidentally brush any wax onto the surrounding surface. If you want a darker finish, simply apply a second coat of tinted wax.

6 Artificially antiquing or ageing the gilding is of course optional. However, a comparison between the antiqued finish shown here and the pre-antiqued finish in step 4 of gold leaf gilding reveals the former to be a more subtle and less "glitzy" finish.

6

A

B *Paints and Glazes*
A Yellow eggshell

C paint.
B Artist's oil: burnt

D sienna. Medium: 1
part scumble glaze, 1

part mineral spirits
(white spirit). Ratios
in glaze: 1 part artist's
oil, 3 parts medium.
C Artist's oil: burnt
umber. Medium: as B

above. Ratios in glaze:
as B above.
D Artist's oil: black.
Medium: as B above.
Ratios in glaze: as B
above.

Tortoiseshell effect

Tortoiseshell simulations are most effective, and realistic, when applied to small decorative objects, such as jewelry boxes and, as shown here, picture frames. Although it is possible to reproduce the finish on larger surface areas, given the (small) size of the original source material, the effect would be little more than a crude pastiche.

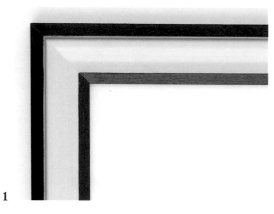

1 To the previously primed and undercoated frame, brush on two coats of black oil paint (gloss paint) to the raised outer and inner perimeters of the moulding, and two coats of yellow eggshell paint A to the curved middle section. Allow to dry for up to 24 hours after each coat.

2 Using a triangle (set square) and a pencil, divide the curved middle of the frame into equal sections, and mark the four diagonal mitred corners. The length of the sections will depend on the size of the frame, but as a rough rule of thumb a 24in (60cm) side should be divided into four 6in (15cm) segments.

3 With a clean rag, wipe a thin coat of scumble glaze over the middle section of one side of the frame.

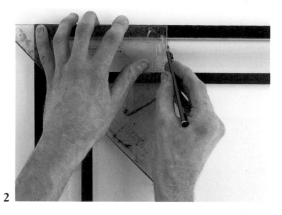

4 Using a small artist's brush, apply pale brown glaze B in random, irregular-shaped patches. The number, and opacity, of the patches varies from section to section. Use the illustration and/or a piece of real tortoiseshell for guidance. Make sure you don't cover the pencil divisions between sections with glaze.

5 Next, apply darker brown glaze C, again using a small artist's brush, to create random, irregular-shaped patches which, in almost all cases, overlap the paler patches established during the previous step 4.

6 Now apply a few patches of black glaze D on top of the paler and darker brown glazes. As with steps 4 and 5, vary the number, shape and size of the patches to give each section of the moulding a distinctive look.

7 Gently flick the bristles of a small badger softener back and forth over the surface to soften and blend the still-wet glazes. Then repeat steps 3-7 along the other three sides of the frame, and allow to dry for 24 hours.

8 Using a small varnishing brush, apply one coat of clear gloss polyurethane varnish to the middle section of the frame. Then allow to dry thoroughly for approximately 24 hours.

9 Using a small artist's brush and a straight edge, apply a thin band of white enamel paint over the pencil lines applied in step 3. (The bands simulate ivory inserts dividing tortoise-shell sections of the frame.)

10 In this example use red eggshell for paint A, while slightly increasing the percentage of medium in glazes B and C, and decreasing the medium and increasing the black pigment in glaze D.

5

6

7

8

9

10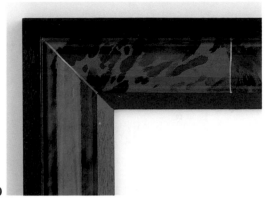

Ageing metal

Exposed to the atmosphere, artefacts and architectural fixtures and fittings made of metals such as bronze, copper, brass, steel (not stainless-steel) and lead are naturally subject to tarnishing and corrosion. The chemical reactions that take place gradually produce a patination over the surface of the metal. Not only can this be aesthetically pleasing, it will also lend the object in question an air of antiquity.

The decorative appeal of naturally patinated metals has been such that painters and craftsman have devised a variety of methods for antiquing new metal surfaces. For example, metalworkers can reproduce the effect of verdigris – a green and white crumbly paste that builds up on the surface of bronze, copper and brass – by treating an object with corrosive acids and subjecting it to high temperatures. While this is a highly toxic and hazardous process that is beyond the scope of the amateur decorator, cold patinating fluids, available from specialist suppliers, can be used as an alternative, and they will produce similar, highly effective results.

Cold patinating fluids are formulated to produce different types of patination depend-ing on the metal to which they are applied. For example, the patinating technique demonstrated on page 134 shows how to blue and blacken a steel candelabrum (an effect that can also be achieved by burying the object in the back garden for a year!). While patinating fluids produce almost instanta-neous results, they are highly toxic and therefore stringent precautions must be taken in order to protect eyes, lungs and exposed areas of skin while handling them.

A less hazardous method of creating metal patina effects not only on metallic surfaces, but also on pottery, wood and plaster, is to simulate them with paints, glazes and pow-ders. For example, in the technique shown on pages 132-3 an ordinary terracotta pot has been "transformed" into an antique bronze artefact that is heavily patinated with verdi-gris. The effect is achieved by simply painting the surface with a metallic bronze paint, prior to applying blue and green water-based glazes and ground chalk (whiting). Similarly, in the patination technique demonstrated on page 135 a brand-new terracotta garden trough has been "converted" into an antique weathered lead plant-holder.

Right:
This 16th-century, Burgundian wrought-iron candlestand is original, but any village blacksmith should be able to produce a copy, which could then be artificially aged by applying a patinating fluid.

Right:
The wrought-iron shutter hinge and the 18th-century brass candlestick are original. As an alternative to ageing modern reproduct-ions with patinating fluid, you could simply bury them in the garden for six months.

Verdigris

id="1"...

A *Pastes and Glazes*

A Powder pigments: 1 part gold powder, 3 parts bronze powder. Medium: clear gloss polyurethane varnish. Ratios in paste: 3 parts pigments, 1 part varnish.

B 1 part deep blue-green latex (matte emulsion) paint, 1 part water.

C 1 part pale blue latex (matte emulsion) paint, 1 part water.

D 1 part pale green latex (matte emulsion) paint, 1 part water.

1 Seal the surface of the terracotta vase by brushing on a mixture of 3 parts white glue (PVA) to 1 part water. Allow the surface to dry for approximately two hours.

2 Using a 2in (5cm) decorator's brush apply two coats of bronze-gold paste A. You should leave the surface to dry for approximately two hours after each coat.

3 With a clean rag, wipe blue-green glaze B over the inside and outside of the vase, varying the density of colour at random over the surface. Then charge the rag with water and drag it around the rim of the vase. The water will run down the sides, producing streaks in the glaze that allow some of the bronze-gold basecoat to show through. Allow to dry for four hours.

4 Using a 1in (2.5cm) artist's brush, apply streaks of pale blue glaze C and pale green glaze D in random, and sometimes overlapping, patches over the inside and outside of the vase. Then dip the brush in water and, as with the rag in step 3, run it around the rim and allow the water to dribble down and produce streaks in the glazes. The more you repeat this process, the more the underlying colours will show through. Allow to dry for four hours.

5 Rub back and blend the glazes with a piece of 0 grade steel (wire) wool. (The extent to which you do this depends on how much you wish to fade the colours.)

5

6

8

6 Mix up a thin antiquing wash of 1 part burnt umber powder pigment to 9 parts of a medium made up of equal quantities of white glue (PVA) and water. Apply this to the surface of the vase with a small decorator's brush and, while the wash is still tacky, wipe ground chalk (whiting) over the surface with a clean dry cloth.

7 Leave small deposits of ground chalk in the decorative moulding under the rim.

8 If the vase is to be exposed to moisture it will need to be sealed with one or two coats of matte or eggshell (satin) clear polyurethane varnish. However, as with weathered lead (*see* page 135), note that the varnish will to some extent tone down the powdery texture of the verdigris, giving it a more reflective finish.

7

The cold patinating fluid used to oxidize metal surfaces – illustrated here on a steel candelabrum – is toxic. It must at all times be kept out of the reach of children, and for your own protection you must wear rubber gloves and goggles and work in a well-ventilated area when applying it. Always follow the manufacturer's instructions on the container.

1 Clean the surface of the steel candelabrum with a cotton ball dipped in a little denatured alcohol (methylated spirits). Allow to dry thoroughly for up to two hours.

2 Working in a well-ventilated area, and wearing protective rubber gloves, rub down the steel surface with a cotton ball soaked in cold patinating fluid.

The fluid acts as an oxidizing agent and will initially blue, and then blacken, the metal.

Metal patination

3 Broadly speaking, the more patinating fluid you apply, and the longer you leave it to act on the surface, the blacker the candelabrum will become.

Once you are happy with the colour, rinse the candelabrum thoroughly in water and, when it has dried off, apply a proprietary fixing agent (available, with instructions, from suppliers of the patinating fluid).

3

1

2

3

4

Paints and Glazes

A 2 parts black latex (matte emulsion) paint, 2 parts white latex (matte emulsion) paint, 1 part burnt umber powder pigment.

B 8 parts black latex

(matte emulsion) paint, 2 parts white latex (matte emulsion) paint, ½ part burnt umber powder pigment.

C 8 parts white latex (matte emulsion) paint, 2 parts black

latex (matte emulsion) paint, ½ part ultramarine powder pigment.

Weathered lead

5

1 To seal the surface of the terracotta trough, brush on a solution of 1 part white glue (PVA) to 1 part water. Allow to dry for two hours.

2 Using a 2in (4cm) decorator's brush, apply two coats of pale gray paint A. Allow approximately four hours drying time after each coat.

3 Again using the small decorator's brush, apply random patches of dark gray glaze B. Then charge a 1in (2.5cm) artist's brush with water and drag it around the rim of the trough, letting the water run down the sides. This will

create streaks in the glaze and allow some of the basecoat to show through. Repeat a few times and allow to dry.

4 Repeat step 3 with off-white glaze C, but apply most of the patches to the upper half of the trough. Once dry, soften and blend the glazes by rubbing them down with 00 grade steel wool.

5 Having brushed on a solution of 1 part white glue (PVA) to 1 part water and allowed it to become tacky, wipe a liberal quantity of pummice powder over the surface using a clean rag.

6 Wipe off excess pumice with the rag, but leave powdery deposits in the crevices of the decorative mouldings. If the trough is to be exposed to

moisture, apply one or two coats of matte or satin clear polyurethane varnish. But *note* that the varnish will produce a less powdery and more reflective finish.

6

Trompe l'oeil

Right:
**Trompe l'oeil
shutters and a *faux*
stone surround
bring a little light
relief to an outside
wall of a house at
Oppede-le-Vieux in
Provence, France.**

Following page:
**A fine example of
trompe l'oeil
woodgrained wall
panelling.**

Right:
**The application of
lighter and darker
versions of the same
basic yellow glaze,
to create
appropriately placed
highlights and
shadows across the
surface, ensures that
this trompe l'oeil
wall panelling takes
on a three-
dimensional
appearance.**

*T*rompe l'oeil translates from the French as "trick of the eye" and is a method of decorative painting in which the artist employs light, shade and perspective to give flat-painted images a three-dimensional appearance. The earliest examples of trompe l'oeil date back to Greek and Roman times. For example, until the end of the 1st century AD, few Roman houses had windows any larger than slits. This meant that there were vast areas of wall to decorate, and so in response painters developed ways to create the illusion of light, space and a "view" of the outside world.

At the ancient Roman town of Pompeii, for example, evidence has been found of wall schemes that included trompe l'oeil columns and scenic views beyond. The "open-air" feeling and the sense of space was further enhanced by painting the upper sections of the walls as sky. Some rooms were even painted in the form of complete gardens and included groups of figures and classical temples. The Roman writer Vitruvius described some of the more glorious and fanciful subjects depicted:

". . . there are harbours, promontories, seashores, rivers, fountains . . . in some places there are also pictures designed in the grand style with figures of gods or detailed mythological episodes, or the battles at Troy or the wanderings of Ulysses with landscape backgrounds."

Roman and Greek trompe l'oeil was studied and copied in Medieval Europe, particularly Italy, with painters working either directly on plaster walls or cloth hangings. Later, during the Renaissance, highly skilled (and often famous) artists were, for the first time, employed to decorate the homes of the nobility, having previously worked solely on religious buildings. At the Palazzo Ducale in Mantua, Italy, for example, a painted room depicts courtiers in groups, massed in the foreground and looking toward the distant hills behind. The illusion visually enlarges the proportions of the room and, as is often the case with trompe l'oeil, includes an element of humour. Anyone standing in the room quickly discovers that they are not the only onlooker present as in the middle of the ceiling above *putti* are depicted peering down over a balustrade at the scene below.

Throughout the Renaissance the Italian style of decoration dominated European design, but by the beginning of the 17th century France had become the arbiter of taste. As the power of the French court turned Baroque style, which had its origins in Italy, into a mainstream influence, Baroque themes abounded in the work of trompe l'oeil artists. The vogue for Chinoiserie was also influential. After the Princess of Orange had the walls of her closet decorated with Chinoiserie panels taken from Oriental lacquer screens, many artists began to imitate the effect in paint, varnishing the work in order to produce a lustrous, glossy sheen.

Left:
The ornate plaster-panelled walls of a bedroom in a mid-19th-century Victorian house have been embellished with *grisaille*. **The flowers and fruit motif was copied from an original French fabric (***c.* **1850s) and applied partly by stencil and partly freehand.**

Left:
The panelled walls of another bedroom in the house shown *opposite*, **have been decorated with stencilled flower and leaf motifs taken from a reproduction of a mid-19th-century French fabric. Additional freehand shading gives the images a three-dimensional quality.**

During the 17th century, the fashion for trompe l'oeil spread to the expanding middle classes throughout Europe and ornate plasterwork and carving was in many instances replaced by wall and ceiling painting. For example, the Grand Staircase at Knole, in Kent, England, painted between 1607-1608 features panels of figurative trompe l'oeil that are edged by *faux* mouldings and balustrading.

By the 18th century, trompe l'oeil had become the height of sophisticated fashion, and once again classical antiquity proved an important influence and inspiration. One of the finest examples of the re-introduction of Etruscan style was the Boudoir of Marie Antoinette at Fontainebleau, France, which was decorated with cloud-painted ceilings around 1787; the workmanship being of an exceptionally high standard.

In Sweden, at this time, trompe l'oeil imitations of carved or cast decoration was most frequently used on ceilings, the designs often being copied from European engravings that had become increasingly available in Scandinavia. Because carving softwoods (the primary source of timber in Scandinavia) is difficult, trompe l'oeil wooden mouldings were plentiful in 17th- and 18th-century Sweden. However, painters did not restrict themselves to imitation carvings. For example, at Olsbodo in Norke a room is hung with a collection of

Above:

In Scandinavia, particularly during the 18th and 19th centuries, it was common practice in lesser dwellings to imitate the lavish decorations found in more opulent manor houses. The trompe l'oeil paintings and accompanying ornate frames decorating the walls of this Swedish farmhouse bedroom were painted by an itinerant craftsman, probably in exchange for food and lodging.

everyday objects; a hat, keyring, bag, brushes, pipe rack and Delft tobacco jar being displayed on a deep apricot background.

As the 18th century drew to a close, trompe l'oeil was often used as the focal point of an entire decorative scheme. For instance, Charles-Louis Clerisseau's elaborate designs for a "ruin room" at S. Trinita dei Monti, in Italy, were entirely dependent on the painted illusion. In this scheme the walls were painted to expose "broken" columns and the ceiling appeared to open to the sky above, with trees peeping through.

In the 19th century, many grander houses were also decorated with trompe l'oeil, often as part of a Historical-Revival scheme, while in the 20th century several well-known artists produced trompe l'oeil work of high quality; the most notable being the English painter, Rex Whistler who was a master of architectural trompe l'oeil.

One of his most famous schemes is a landscape in the Map Room at Port Lympne, in Kent, England, which features buildings, a lake and a stonework arch flanked by figures on the walls, while the barrel-vault ceiling above is draped in striped tenting – all executed in paint. Another scheme at Plas Newydd, Anglesey, Wales, is widely regarded as his most perfect work. A romantic Italian townscape, it includes mountains and buildings. One special feature in the foreground at one corner of the room is an arcade which

appears to stretch away from an archway painted on the end wall.

Trompe l'oeil also began to appear in more modest homes during the 20th century. In the 1930s, for example, the English painter Eric Ravilious treated the panels of folding doors as windows and created a vista of a garden with a tennis court, all inside a London apartment. Many anonymous painters thereafter have followed his example of using trompe l'oeil to bring an illusion of space, light and greenery into relatively cramped and sometimes gloomy city homes.

Usually painted in colour, trompe l'oeil can also be executed *en grisaille*. Grisaille is a traditional technique for producing three-dimensional effects using tones of gray (hence its name, from the French *gris*), although tones of brown, blue and green can also be employed. Most frequently used as a frieze around a room and as wall panelling, as well as to suggest wall niches displaying statuary, grisaille was used extensively in many period Scandinavian and European interiors from the 17th century onward.

Like all trompe l'oeil work, grisaille demands of the painter a degree of artistic skill and an understanding of the principles and application of light, shade and perspective to produce the desired effect. A step-by-step introduction to this technique, showing how to create a grisaille panel on a cupboard door, is given on pages 144-5.

Right:

The decorations in this bedroom in a house in Devon, England, are a pastiche of an interior in an 18th-century Italian villa. The trompe l'oeil panelling was painted in four shades of blue, and contrasted with the trompe l'oeil painted plaster mouldings in the frieze above. The picture panels were "framed" with freehand-painted wreaths.

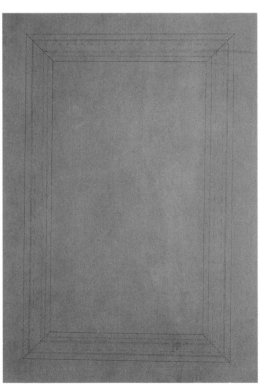

Paints and Glazes

A Blue-gray latex (matte emulsion) paint.

B 3 parts blue-gray latex (matte emulsion) paint, 1 part black latex (matte emulsion) paint.

C 1 part blue-gray latex (matte emulsion) paint, 3 parts black latex (matte emulsion) paint.

D 1 part blue-gray latex (matte emulsion) paint, 3 parts white latex (matte emulsion) paint.

A monochrome form of trompe l'oeil, grisaille is a traditional technique employing light, shade and perspective to deceive the onlooker into believing he or she is looking at a three-dimensional object rather than a flat, painted surface. To be convincing it requires a degree of artistic ability. However, careful copying of the simple wall panel shown here will familiarize you with the principles involved and enable you to tackle other architectural features or, for the more adventurous, decorative subjects such as flowers, vases, nymphs and cherubs.

Grisaille

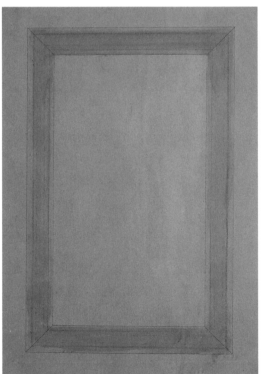

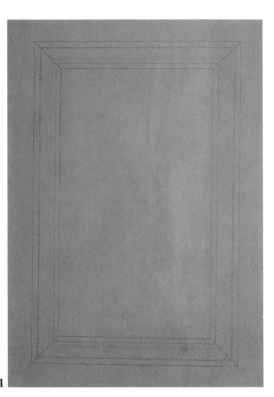

1 Apply two coats of blue-gray paint A over the walls and allow them to dry. Then faintly mark out the external and internal perimeters and the four mitred corners of the frame, using a pencil, a straight edge and a spirit-level. (*Note:* The moulding is a simulation of the one used for the tortoiseshell effect on pages 128-9. If possible, keep a section of the moulding you're copying to hand, for reference, while working.)

Next, mark the inner perimeter of the raised flat section of moulding that runs around the outside of the frame. Then mark the inner perimeter of the chamfered section of moulding that runs around the inside of the frame.

2 Finish outlining the shape of the moulding by applying two faint dotted lines to mark the highest and lowest points of the curved middle section of the frame.

3 Next, mix up a thin blue-gray wash by diluting 1 part paint A with 6 parts water, and brush it out over the outline of the frame using a 2in (5cm) standard decorator's brush. The pencil guidelines should remain visible through the translucent wash.

4 If this was a real frame the predominant light source (here, above the top left of the frame at approximately 10 o'clock) would reflect off its surface, producing highlights on the raised sections and areas most exposed to it and shadows in the recesses and other areas least exposed to it.

Begin by copying the mid-tone shadows. As you can see, the position and width of the shadows varies on each side of the frame. However, the basic method of application is the same for each one:

Dampen the tip of a swordliner brush with a little water and dip it into paint B. Position a straight edge (with two blocks of wood attached to the back of each end to hold it just proud of the surface) over the appropriate pencil line, and drag the paint over the surface. Thin shadows can be completed with a single drag; thicker shadows will need more than one application, and the straight edge will have to be moved over the pencil line that marks the other side of the shadow.

After completing a shadow, dip the brush in a little water and go over it again to soften the edges. This is

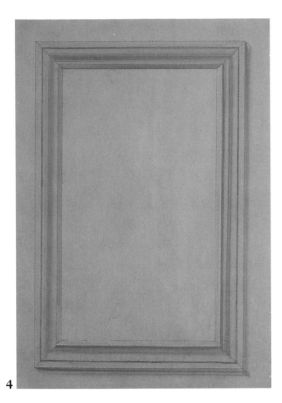

4

5

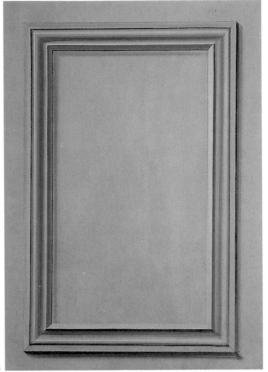

6

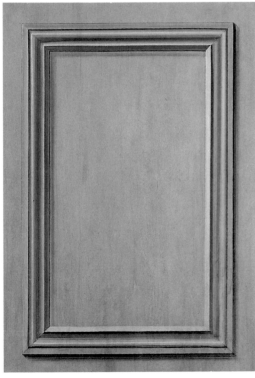

8

6 Apply the high-lights, using paint D and, once again, soften them into the surrounding shadows.

7 The subtle contrasts between different depths of shadow, and the stronger contrast between the shadows and highlights, gives the flat, painted frame a three-dimensional appearance.

8 Once the paint has dried, mix up a thin antiquing wash consisting of 1 part paint B, 20 parts water and a touch of burnt umber powder pigment, and brush it over the frame and wall.

especially important with the thicker shadows. You must work quickly, as the water-based paint soon dries.

5 Next, employing the same method and paint C, apply the darker shadows. In most cases this

involves going over sections of the mid-tone shadows to darken them and then softening the edges with water to subtly blend them into the lighter mid-tones.

7

Wallpaper

Above left:

The "Thrush and Storks" paper in the South Bedroom of Temple Newsam, in England, is a reproduction of a late 19th-century design, possibly copied from an even earlier paper.

Above right:

A classical laurel wreath motif in gold on cream graces the walls of a Regency period dining room.

$\mathcal{T}$he forerunners of the wallpaper manufacturers were European medieval printers who created religious illustrations which could be pasted onto the wall. These were printed either on textiles or paper using wood engravings, and although the results were often crude, the technique employed did allow for repeat patterns to be made.

By the 15th century a substantial increase in the availability of paper coincided with a desire by the poorer classes to find a less expensive substitute for the sumptuous textile wall-hangings favoured by the rich. This demand encouraged the early printers to produce simple decorative paper panels.

For the most part, 16th-century wallpaper designs emulated either textiles in damask and flamestitch and floral designs, or mural painting. The early manufacturers of wallpaper also printed the decorative title pages of books; the black and white heraldic papers produced being used to line deed-boxes and chests as well as for binding books. However, there is little evidence today of coloured papers being widely available at this time, although a few very crudely coloured examples have been found.

By the 17th century the French *dominotiers* were becoming expert in imitating fabrics on paper. The writer Savary des Bruslons noted that "a dominotier makes a type of tapestry on paper . . . which is used by the poorer classes in Paris to cover the walls of their huts or their shops." The papers of this period, whether produced in France or in England, fell into two distinct categories. First, the simple pattern repeat, which was usually geometric and printed from one wood block, and second, more complicated designs, such as shields, vases or flowers, which were created from several blocks. The designs were first printed in black onto the paper and then coloured size was applied using a type of stencil.

It is interesting to note that at this time wallpaper was not pasted directly onto the wall but, generally, onto linen. The linen was then either secured to the wall with copper tacks or attached to wooden battens which were fixed to the wall. Also, there was a substantial difference in quality between various types of early wallpaper. The more costly papers were produced from carefully carved new wooden blocks, printed meticulously and sensitively coloured. However, there was also

Right:

The combination of distressed dark green and red-brown painted Lincrusta below dado, and typical late 19th-century printed papers above, are immediately evocative of Victorian style. Note how the gilt-framed print in the hall "picks up" the colours in the paper behind it and "lifts" the darker Lincrustas below.

a growing market for less expensive papers. These were printed, without much skill, from worn blocks and sold to the less wealthy members of the community at rural fairs.

In England, the most important technological advance that took place during the 17th century was the introduction of flock wallpaper. (Flock is the small shearing of wool left over in the manufacture of cloth.) The process involved painting the background colour onto the paper or canvas, then printing or stencilling the design onto it with an adhesive. Finally the flock was scattered over the adhesive, producing a velvet-like pile over the chosen design. Although flock wallpaper first appeared in the 17th century, the golden period for the product was 1715-1745, when papers of exceptional quality were produced in England (and exported to France).

The end of the 17th century saw another technological advance, when sheets of paper were glued together and, for the first time, sold in rolls. Moreover, the painted or printed pattern could be devised to conceal the joins and, as a result, more adventurous designs were produced. However, it did mean that 18th-century paper hangers had to be more skilled than their predecessors.

By the beginning of the 18th century, black and white papers had virtually disappeared in Europe, the demand for coloured papers having been stimulated by the importation, from the end of the 17th century, of vividly coloured Chinese papers hand-painted with birds, trees, pagodas and sometimes Chinese figures in landscapes. Indeed, the trade with the Far East was one of the major influences on interior decoration in the 18th century. Holland and England had secured highly prized trade routes with China; the ships bringing back cargoes of exotic spices and tea along with porcelain, lacquerwork, silks, screens and hand-painted wallpaper. The papers found their way into manor houses, palaces and chateaux all over Europe. They were usually applied in panels, sometimes edged with gilt filets, as at Nostell Priory in England.

As the obsession with Chinese taste spread, the designs were copied by European painters, who produced flamboyant chinoiseries or visions of China, with varying degrees of accuracy. After the Chinese originals, the French papers were the most sought-after. The French even created a new category in their Royal Inventories, known as: "*Divers ouvrages de la Chine*".

Although wallpaper was used in grand houses in the early 18th century, it is most likely that these "paper wall-hangings", as

they were known at the time, were used in minor rooms, while fabric continued to be used in the principal salons. Even so, the use of wallpaper became so widespread that from 1712 the English government levied a tax on paper "printed, painted or stained to serve for hangings".

Most 18th-century wallpapers were inspired by textiles; manufacturers boasting of their abilities to emulate damasks, velvets and needlework. One of the major figures in wallpaper design during this period was John Baptist Jackson. Born in 1700, he became a pupil of the engraver Kirkhall and then travelled to Paris around 1725. There he came into contact with the young Papillon, a famous French paper-stainer, before moving on to Italy, where he became interested in the Italian Renaissance art of chiaroscuro. In 1746 he returned to England, determined to revive English wallpaper manufacturing, and subsequently became one of the principal designers of distemper-printed wallpaper in the late 18th century.

The French wallpaper industry was so well-established by the last quarter of the 18th century that one manufacturer, Jean-Baptiste Reveillon, became a "Manufacture Royale". (Dufour and Zuber were also held in high regard.) By this stage, France had overtaken England as the major European producer of wallpaper and their leading manufacturers, noted for paying their designers extremely well, expended considerable effort producing specialist papers on commission for the homes of the nobility. However, it should be noted that the practice of printing in distemper colours led, by the middle of the 18th century, to a decrease in the quality of papers. And it was not until the 1780s that the quality improved sufficiently to do justice to the excellent patterns that the designers were producing.

Despite the fact that innovations in colour printing techniques were underway during this period, in England much wallpaper continued to be laboriously hand-coloured on the wall, possibly to outwit the exciseman. (In 1778 the excise officers were instructed to search out this heinous fraud.) However, hand-painted wallpaper seems to have fallen from fashion by the end of the 18th century, and despite revivals in America and France in

Left:

The wallpaper in the Prince's Room in Temple Newsam, England, is a reproduction of the original paper hung here by Lady Hertford in 1827, and is in keeping with the magnificent Regency four-poster bed.

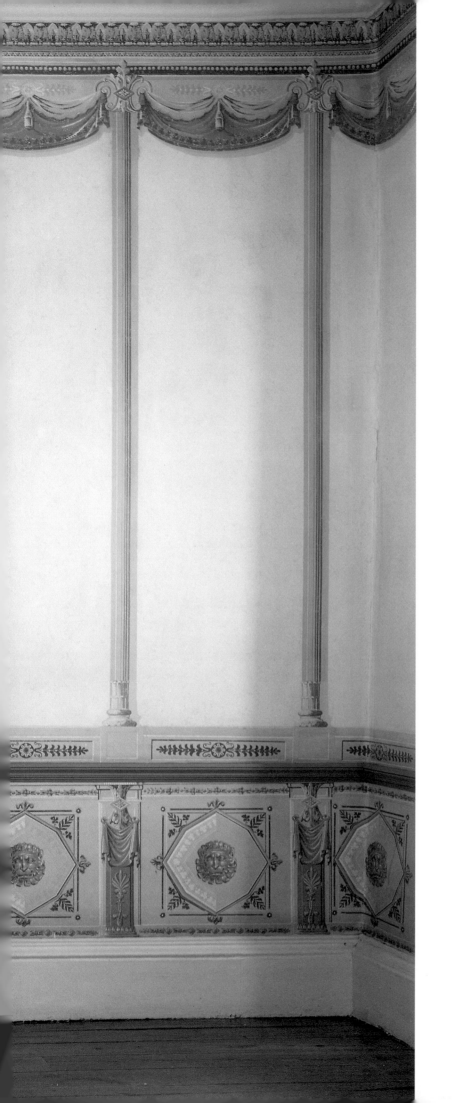

Left:
The "Colonnade" wallpaper (from Toynbee-Clarke Interiors) in the hallway of the Jumel mansion was reproduced from the original paper brought back from France – like the paper shown *above* – by Jumels in 1826.

Above:
A reproduction of an early 19th-century French document wallpaper, in the Jumel mansion in Harlem, New York. (The *lit-bateau* was given to Jumels in 1826 by Princess Hortense and was, supposedly, used by Napoleon when he was First Consul of the French Republic.)

the 1840s, no such corresponding revival took place in England.

By 1773 the English wallpaper industry was sufficiently strong (its papers were by now being exported in large quantities all over the world) for the Government of the day to open up the market by repealing the Act of Parliament that had banned the importation of foreign papers, while imposing a customs duty of 1d – although the East India Company was exempt.

In England, the early 19th century saw ever-increasing taxation on wallpaper. Indeed, the industry was seen as a very important source of revenue by the government; so much so that in 1806 the falsification of wallpaper stamps was added to the list of offences punishable by death. One consequence of the high tax levy was that English manufacturers, in an attempt to increase their sales, began to concentrate on simple, inexpensive designs that would appeal to the mass market. (As a result, the wonderful scenic papers that date from the early 19th century tend to be French in origin.)

In France, by the 1830s, the quality of wallpaper was of such a high standard that many writers declared that it was quite wasteful to use silk on the walls as paper had an equally pleasing look. Many quite outrageous trompe l'oeil wallpapers were produced that simulated draped and swagged fabrics – although, in fact, this effect had been used as early as 1720 in England, when William Kent hung wallpaper instead of draped velvet in the saloon of Kensington Palace, London.

The middle of the 19th century saw further developments in the industry. After approximately 1835, wallpapers were applied directly onto plaster, instead of being pasted onto canvas and then fixed to the wall with a batten system. And while increased mechanization from the 1840s led to a glut of small repeat patterns on the market, the lifting of taxation in 1836 encouraged designers to produce florid, overcomplicated patterns, which became a feature of High Victorian style. (They also introduced, for the first time, papers designed specifically for the nursery. Some early examples show design of the period at its worst, but charming children's wallpapers did appear later in the century.)

Right:

Some of the early wallpapers were produced in the patterns of the traditional silk damasks that covered walls before the advent of paper. Colours were usually deep blues, reds or greens. Such designs are still produced by manufacturers today.

Above:

Chinoiserie-influenced paper is matched to the fabric swagged at the window. Throughout the centuries rich patterns from the East have influenced fabric as well as wallpaper designs. Today, many firms reproduce matching fabrics and papers in period patterns.

By the late 19th century, designers like William Morris began to react against the excesses of the mid-century. Their intention was to restore good taste and re-establish quality workmanship. Morris was enormously influential, both in his insistence on the use of the purest colours and techniques and, perhaps more importantly, in his attention to the actual design. His influence, along with that of the designer, and author of *The Grammar of Ornament*, Owen Jones, can be seen in the hundreds of tasteful mass-produced papers manufactured during the last two decades of the 19th century. These papers were produced in three interrelated patterns for the traditional tri-partite wall treatment of dado, field and frieze. For the area below the dado, particularly in hallways, heavy embossed papers – anaglyptas and Lincrusta – were developed and designed to be painted. (A technique for "ageing" Lincrusta paper is illustrated on page 158.)

While the tri-partite division remained popular after 1900, walls gradually became less elaborately decorated, although the decorative frieze was retained. Traditional designs depicting, for example, birds and flowers, could still be found, along with neo-Adam chinoiserie and rococo patterns. But by end of the 1920s "futurist" and "cubist" patterns had arrived on the market, and thereafter both modern and traditional patterns, catering for every taste and purse have been widely available. (Ironically, however, the mass market for wallpaper produced a reaction among an "elite", who came to regard paper as an inferior option and reverted to using fabrics (such as silk) and traditional paint finishes and effects.

Today, whichever period style you wish to re-create, you should be able to find an appropriate "document" wallpaper reproduced by leading manufacturers from their extensive archives. (A list of manufacturers and suppliers appears on pages 172-175.)

Right:

This "prohibitively expensive" "Chinese Garden" paper was hand-painted circa 1800 and hung in Temple Newsam in 1927-28. It is embellished with images taken from the first volume of Audubon's "Birds of America".

Overleaf:

In the 19th century hard-wearing embossed papers were produced for the lower division of the wall. Jonathan Hudson aged and distressed new Lincrusta panels (still produced to the original patterns) in this 19th-century house to add to the period mood.

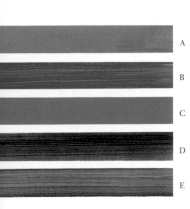

A eggshell paint.
D Artist's oils: 5 parts Aubuisson green, 3 parts Prussian blue, 1 part raw umber, 1 part black. Medium: 1 part transparent oil glaze, 3 parts mineral spirits (white spirit).
E Ratios in glaze: 4 parts artist's oils, 1 part medium.
E Artist's oils: 4 parts burnt umber, 1 part black. Medium: transparent oil glaze. Ratios in glaze: 4 parts artist's oils, 1 part medium.

Paints and Glazes

A Sage green latex (matte emulsion) paint.
B Gray-green eggshell paint.
C Bronze-gold

1

2

Ageing Lincrusta

1 Using a standard decorator's brush, apply two coats of sage green paint **A** to the wall above the dado strip, two coats of gray-green paint **B** to the dado and skirting (base-board) mouldings, and two coats of bronze-gold paint **C** to the embossed Lincrusta paper. Allow the latter to dry for 12 hours after each coat. (*Note:* The Lincrusta, dado and skirting should have been previously primed and undercoated.)

3

2 Having protected the top of the skirting moulding with a strip of low-tack masking tape, apply one coat of blue-green glaze **D** over the Lincrusta, using a 4in (10cms) decorator's brush.

3 Using a clean dry rag, gently wipe off some of the glaze from the raised sections of Lincrusta to create highlights that contrast with the darker accumulation of glaze in the recessed areas. Keep turning the rag, and replace it once it becomes clogged with glaze. Allow the surface to dry for 24 hours.

4 Brush on antiquing glaze **E** over the Lincrusta, as in step 2.

6

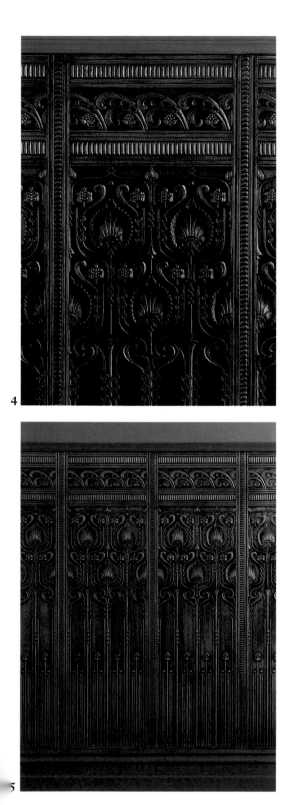

4

5

5 Repeat step 3, but this time wipe off some glaze from the recessed sections as well as the raised areas. For an authentic finish the darkest accumulations of glaze should remain in the narrow recesses least exposed to light and most likely to accumulate dirt.

6 Remove the masking tape and wipe off any glaze that might have crept onto the skirting with mineral spirits (white spirit).

Print room

The fashion for decorating rooms with prints pasted onto wallpapered or painted walls (usually white, or straw-coloured) first became popular in the 1750s. Jean Michel Papillon's detailed illustrations (c.1759), intended for inclusion in Diderot and d'Alembert's *Encyclopedie*, show walls covered with small framed engravings, while Horace Walpole, in his *Description of the Villa at Strawberry Hill* (published 1784), writes of a room "hung with yellow paper and prints, framed in a new manner, invented by Lord Cardigan, that is with black and white borders". The choice of subjects of the prints varied from Old Masters and ancestral portraits to etchings of stately homes and churches and risqué or politically satirical drawings by painters and engravers such as Hogarth.

While many Print Rooms, such as those at Strawberry Hill in Twickenham, and The Vyne in Hampshire, England, featured black and white prints and borders simply pasted to the walls, others were more flamboyantly decorated, with trompe l'oeil paper cut-outs of bows, swags, garlands and chains "supporting" and embellishing the prints. Thomas Chippendale decorated rooms in this manner at The Hatch, in Kent, in 1762, and charged the not inconsiderable sum of £14.10s.0d for labour and £8.9s.10d for materials, which included: 506 printed borders; 106 printed festoons; 91 printed corners; 11 bustos; 18 satyrs and lion masks; 39 rings and 12 masks; 74 knots and 28 baskets and 8 sheets of chains.

Initially popular in England, Ireland and France, Print Rooms also appeared in grander North American homes, particularly in the Southern States. The decorative convention continued well into the 19th century, when it was sometimes extended to hallways and corridors, and has recently enjoyed a revival led by interior designers using commercially available books of prints and borders specifically designed for the purpose (*see* page 174).

Left:
A trompe l'oeil print room effect in an early 19th-century London apartment – images of animals and reptiles are quite common themes.

Above and overleaf:
Two trompe l'oeil print rooms; above in the dressing room of a London town house, and overleaf at Kenwood House, London.

7

Print effect

1

1 Using a photo-copy machine with an enlarging and reducing facility, photostat the prints and borders – increasing or reducing their size from that of the source material accordingly. (*Note:* For the best results, use a good quality paper.) Then, carefully tape the photostats onto a flat surface, such as a cutting board.

The prints and accompanying borders used to illustrate the print room technique shown here are re-sized photostats taken from a compilation of 18th- and 19th-century originals reproduced in book form. For suppliers of this and other similar compilations, refer to the Directory on pages 172-5.

2 Brew up some tea or coffee, let it cool down, and then brush it out over a spare piece of photocopy paper and allow to dry. Experiment with the brew until you are happy with the colour, and then brush it out over the prints and borders. (In this case, a paler brew was applied to the print and a darker one to the border.)

2

3

4

3 Once the paper has dried, carefully remove the masking tape and stick the borders in position on the wall with PVA white glue.

You can either match your wall colour to the one shown here, or experiment with alternative eggshell or latex (emulsion) coloured back-grounds.

In this example the borders and prints are the same size, and are evenly spaced horizontally across the wall. However, you may wish to experiment with different sizes, positions and spacings.

4 Cut out the prints to the appropriate size using a craft knife and a straight edge, and then carefully stick them in position within their respective borders.

5 Once the glue has dried thoroughly, you can apply a coat of matte or satin clear polyurethane varnish for protection. It is particularly important to do this if the prints and borders are likely to be subjected to either moisture or excessive wear and tear.

6 Alternatively, you can age the prints by brushing on a coat of an antiquing wash consisting of – artist's oils: 3 parts burnt umber, 1 part black. Medium: 3 parts transparent oil glaze, 2 parts mineral spirits (white spirit). Ratios in wash: 1 part pigments, 40 parts medium.

7 A final, and recommended, alternative is to reduce the colour contrast between the prints and the background by applying the antiquing wash over the entire surface.

5

6

Materials, equipment and techniques

*T*he following section lists and describes the various items of equipment and the paints, glazes, washes and other materials that you will need to produce the decorative finishes and effects illustrated throughout the book. Information is also supplied on how to prepare different surfaces for decoration.

The section begins with a description of the various brushes you will need to purchase. While good quality brushes are relatively expensive, they invariably produce better results than low-priced alternatives. They also last longer, provided you look after them properly.

Information on brushes is followed by a list of the various items of additional equipment you will need. This includes everything from paint kettles to palette knives, marine sponges to masking tape and sandpaper to stencils. You are advised to make sure that you have the specified equipment to hand before embarking on any particular decorative project, rather than have to go out and buy it halfway through.

Next, a description of proprietary paints and pigments, solvents and mediums and stains and varnishes, and their suitability for different surfaces, is accompanied by explanations of how to mix your own paints, glazes and washes. All the materials and equipment described is readily available from do-it-yourself stores, artists' suppliers or specialist decorating outlets (*see* the Directory).

Penultimately, there is a description of the additional materials you will require for certain finishes. These include items such as transfer metal leaf, metallic powders, patinating fluids and various pastes and powders.

The section concludes with a detailed explanation of how to prepare different types of surfaces prior to decoration. Never underestimate the importance of this preparatory stage. The condition of the underlying surface always has a major effect upon the durability and successful appearance, or otherwise, of any decorative finish.

Finally, it is important to note that some of the materials you will be using, particularly certain pigments, powders and fluids, are highly toxic and/or inflammable. The manufacturers of such products usually supply relevant information on the container, and you should always heed any warnings that are given. Even if you only suspect that a particular material might be toxic, always protect your eyes with goggles, your hands with chemical-resistant gloves and your lungs with a respiratory (or dust) mask when handling it.

Left:
A variety of well-finished surfaces. For results like this, adopt a diligent approach to preparation – it always pays off in the long run.

Equipment

BRUSHES

Artist's brushes:
Round- or flat-bristled, artist's brushes are available in a variety of sizes and qualities. Sable brushes are the most expensive, but are best for fine-detailed freehand work, such as for veining *faux* marble.

Badger softeners:
Badger-hair softening brushes are designed for gently softening and blending still-wet oil-based glazes and water colours initially applied with other brushes, sponges or rags. They come in a variety of sizes – the fan and pencil badger being used for more detailed work. Only the tips of the bristles are used to caress the glazes into the desired finish. Because badger softeners, particularly the bigger ones used for working on larger surface areas, are very expensive, many painters and decorators use either a dusting brush or a hog's hair softener as a substitute. However, in inexperienced hands, the results are unlikely to be as good. Cared for properly, badger softeners will provide many years of service and are, on balance, worth the investment if you envisage doing a lot of specialist decorating.

Dusting brushes:
Also known as jamb dusters, these soft-bristled brushes are used mainly for removing dust from surfaces before applying paints, glazes and varnishes. However, they can also be successfully doubled-up as either dragging brushes or softening and blending brushes if you don't have access to a badger softener.

Fitches:
Hog's hair or white lily bristle fitches are available in a variety of sizes and shapes – either oval, flat or angled. These brushes are primarily used for relatively small-scale applications of oil- and water-based paints and glazes. A coarser-textured angled fitch is particularly useful for spattering glazes over surfaces when antiquing (although an inexpensive substitute is an old toothbrush, which can also be used to good effect for this purpose), and

for cutting-in work when painting the glazing bars of windows.

Flogging brushes:
The coarse, long-bristled, horsehair flogger is available in a variety of sizes. It is primarily used for lightly tapping up and down over surfaces to remove small flecks of wet glaze, and thereby producing the fine surface pores characteristic of various woodgrains, notably oak. However, like standard decorator's brushes and jamb dusters, it can also be used for dragging wet glazes to produce the parallel or wavy "stripes" characteristic of the figuring of many woods – although for finely detailed graining, professionals will usually use a spalter (mottler) brush to create this effect.

Hog's hair softeners:
Made for softening and blending wet oil-based glazes, the hog's hair softener is a lot less costly than a badger softener. However, because its bristles are of a coarser texture, it is harder to use, and in inexperienced hands more likely to produce "cruder" results.

Spalters (Mottlers):
Made from sable or hog's or squirrel hair, spalters (mottlers) are available in a range of sizes and are used by professional grainers for dragging water- or oil-based glazes to simulate the parallel or wavy "stripes" that are so characteristic of the figuring of many species of wood.

Squirrelhead mop:
A fine-bristled dusting brush is particularly useful for gently removing excess metallic powder from surfaces when gilding.

Standard decorator's brushes:
Available in sizes ranging from ½ in (1.25cm) to 6in (15cm), standard decorator's brushes are mainly used to apply primers, undercoats and flat-oil, eggshell and latex (emulsion) paints.
They can also be used for flogging and dragging, but they will produce "cruder" results than the specialist brushes that are intended for such work.

Stencilling brushes:
Stiff-bristled stencilling brushes come in a variety of sizes and are used, as their name implies, to pounce paints and glazes through the cut-out shapes in stencil cards onto an underlying surface. The advantage of a stencil brush is that, being designed to hold only a small quantity of paint or glaze, it encourages a gradual and controlled build-up of colour through the stencil, and minimizes the risk of paint or glaze creeping behind the stencil card and ruining the finish. On the other hand, stencil brushes make stencilling over large areas (such as a repeat border around four walls) a laborious and time-consuming business. Consequently, for speed and ease of application professionals will often use small sponges or rags instead.

Swordliners:
Available in various sizes, swordliner brushes are primarily used, sometimes in conjunction with a straight edge, to produce straight lines of colour (lining) when painting on walls or furniture, as in the Grisaille technique (see pages 144-5). However, they can also be used instead of artist's brushes or feathers for creating vein-like broken lines when marbling.

Varnishing brushes:
Thin, flat-bristled varnishing brushes – known as gliders – are best for applying thin coats of varnish that need a lot of brushing out. Larger flat and oval-shaped varnishing brushes are designed for applying thicker coats of varnish that need less brushing out. Both types have more fine bristles to the square inch or centimetre than standard decorator's brushes, and thereby facilitate a smoother, brush-mark-free application.
Varnishing brushes should never be used to apply paint. However well they are cleaned afterward, flecks of dried paint will almost invariably emerge the next time that you apply a varnish; these will stick to the surface and spoil the look of the finish.
You should always clean varnishing brushes very carefully after use (as instructed below).

Cleaning brushes:
By using the following method for cleaning and storing brushes after use, you will help to preserve their original condition and avoid subsequent problems (and disappointments) the next time you use them.
1 If you have been using water-based paints, glazes and varnishes, move straight on to step 2.
To remove oil-based paints, glazes and varnishes, begin by throroughly cleaning the bristles in a container of mineral spirits (white spirit) or a commercial brush cleaner (some of which are specifically designed for dissolving polyurethane varnishes). Keep changing the spirits as and when necessary, until all traces of colour have been removed from the bristles. And, if possible, avoid getting solvent into the stock of the brush as this will eventually result in the bristles dropping out. (For this reason, you should try to avoid getting paint, glaze or varnish into the top of the bristles, where they enter the stock, in the first place.) Now move on to step 3.
2 If you have been using water-based paints and glazes, immediately clean the brush in a mild solution of warm water and soap. Do not used detergents on your brushes as they will almost certainly strip the bristle of their natural oils and dry them out.
3 When all traces of paint, glaze or varnish have been removed from the bristles, rinse them thoroughly in cold running water.
4 After rinsing, you should remove as much water as possible from the bristles by shaking the brush vigorously.
5 To stop the bristles splaying out as they dry, you should gently fold a sheet of plain paper around them, holding it in place with an elastic band wound around the stock of the brush.
6 Finally, lay the brush on its side, or supported bristles-up, and leave it to dry away from any direct source of heat and at normal room temperature.

ADDITIONAL EQUIPMENT

Artist's palette:
Use an artist's palette, made from

either varnished wood, plastic or disposable waterproof paper on a cardboard base, when working on a decorative finish in which only small quantities of pigment and medium need to be mixed.

Combs:
You can use decorator's combs for dragging glazes to simulate the figuring of various woods when creating authentic or fantasy woodgraining. The combs are available in steel, plastic, rubber and oiled-card, and a variety of sizes – a rocker comb, for example, is specifically designed for simulating the heart grain figuring characteristic of pine. You can, of course, also cut your own combs from sheets of oiled-card and cardboard.

Cotton swabs (buds):
Keep a supply of cotton swabs to hand when producing finely detailed finishes (such as marbling or woodgraining). They will be needed for removing unwanted traces of paint and glaze from surfaces.

Craft knife:
Use a craft knife (or a scalpel) for cutting out "home-made" stencils, cutting masking (drafting) tape, trimming wallpaper and texturing a decorator's sponge.

Dust sheets:
Use cotton, in preference to plastic, dust sheets for protecting floors, furniture and fabrics from accidental splashes or spills of paint and glaze.

Erasers:
Soft erasers are used to rub out pencil outlines, and you should purchase a hard-edged plastic eraser to manipulate the wet glazes into vein-like broken lines when carrying out the Black and gold marbling (see pages 110-1).

Face masks:
Given the toxicity of many pigments and solvents (almost always indicated on the side of the container) you are advised to wear a commercially available respiratory face mask to protect your lungs from noxious fumes when mixing paints, glazes and washes.
And you should wear a mask to prevent you from breathing in dust when you are repairing and keying surfaces prior to decoration.

Feathers:
As an alternative to artist's brushes (or hard-edged erasers) you can use feathers to manipulate the glazes into vein-like broken lines when marbling.

Gloves:
Chemical-resistant gloves must be used to protect your hands when using caustic metal patinating fluids and mixing limewash. Given the toxicity of many pigments and solvents, you are also advised to wear them when mixing paints and glazes and cleaning brushes. Avoid using ordinary household gloves, as they tend to disintegrate when exposed to mineral spirits (white spirit) and caustic fluids.

Masking (drafting) tape:
Use masking tape, available in various widths, to protect areas adjacent to the one you are working on from overspills of paint and glaze, and to mark out the position of grout lines when stoneblocking (see pages 118-9). If you can get hold of it, a low-tack masking tape is preferable to the "stickier" variety, as it is less likely to pull off underlying paint when it is removed. If low-tack tape is unavailable, you can make ordinary masking tape less adhesive by rubbing it back and forth over a tee-shirt or overalls before sticking it to the surface.

Mixing containers:
You may need to buy up to six or seven alloy or plastic paint kettles for preparing the various paints and glazes required for some decorative finishes (*see* Mixing glazes, pages 166-7). Paint kettles come in a variety of sizes, but those with a capacity of between one and two litres (¼-½ gallon) each are best. You will also find it useful to have a number of old saucers and jam jars to hand for mixing smaller quantities of glaze, and a large plastic bucket with a capacity of approximately 10 litres (2 gallons) for tinting large quantities of latex (emulsion) or oil-based eggshell.

Paint tray:
A metal or plastic paint tray serves as a useful container for paints and glazes while you are working. You can press the bristles of your brush or your sponge against the raised inner section of the tray to remove excess paint or glaze before applying it to a surface.

Palette knives:
Purchase one or two palette knives for mixing pigments, solvents and mediums. They are particularly useful for mixing small quantities of glaze on an artist's palette.

Pencils:
Use soft lead pencils for outlining work when stoneblocking (see pages 144-5) or when creating trompe l'oeil or grisaille effects (see pages 118-9). You will also need to purchase a graphite stick for rubbing over the back of tracing paper when transferring the outline of a motif onto oiled stencil card (see pages 54-5).

Plasterer's float:
Use a steel or plastic plasterer's float to apply a thin skim of finishing plaster when producing a distressed plaster finish. You can also use the float to repair larger patches of damaged plaster when making good wall surfaces prior to decoration (*see* Preparing surfaces).

Plumb line:
As an alternative to using a large spirit-level, which may be unwieldly, use a plumb line to assist with the marking-out of true vertical lines when stoneblocking, when setting up repeat stencil motifs down walls, or before applying wallpaper.

Protective goggles:
You must always wear plastic goggles to protect eyes from accidental splashes of caustic fluids. This is particularly important when applying metal patinating fluids (see page 134) or when mixing limewash (see page 168).
Goggles are also useful for keeping paint out of the eyes when decorating ceilings, or for keeping dust at bay when repairing plaster or sanding down surfaces prior to decoration.

Rags:
You will need a plentiful supply of rags to hand when decorating. They should be made of lint-free cotton (available in bundles or sheet-form from specialist decorating and fabric suppliers). Rags that are not lint-free tend to leave fibres on surfaces (especially wet glazes) and will spoil the look of the finished work.

Warning: Never put used paint- or solvent-saturated rags into a sealed plastic bag.
Stored in this way, they have been known to spontaneously combust!

Sandpaper:
You can buy sandpaper in various grades – fine, medium and coarse – and in sheet or block form. Use it for rubbing down and smoothing out surfaces prior to the application of primers and undercoats, as well as for cutting back paint and varnish when antiquing in order to simulate scuffing and wear and tear.

Spoons:
Keep two or three wooden or metal spoons to hand when decorating. They are useful for measuring out quantities of pigment and medium and for mixing paints and glazes.

Spirit-level:
Use a large spirit-level to measure true horizontals when marking out a grid on a surface for stoneblocking. You can also use it instead of a plumb line in order to establish the true verticals.

Sponges:
Purchase one or two natural marine sponges for sponging work. Don't be tempted to use the sort of synthetic sponge intended for washing autos. Unlike a marine sponge they have a flat, uniformly patterned surface unsuitable for creating the random displacement of glaze necessary for an authentic-looking finish. As an alternative to the marine sponge, you could buy a synthetic decorator's sponge, chamfer its edges with a craft knife and texture its smooth surface by ripping out small, randomly spaced pieces of sponge with the tips of a pair of scissors.

Steel (wire) wool:
Use steel (wire) wool in combination with paint stripper for preparing metal surfaces prior to decoration. Being more flexible than sandpaper, steel wool is also useful for keying and smoothing wooden mouldings (eg. on furniture) prior to the application of paint, glaze and varnish, and for cutting-back when antiquing to simulate scuffing and general wear and tear. Use coarser grades of steel wool (0-3) for keying and antiquing. Use finer grades (000-0) for smoothing down prior to waxing, see marbling, pages 112-3.

Steel spatula:
Purchase a steel spatula (wallpaper scraper) for removing old wallpaper and "live" plaster prior to repair and redecoration.

Steel tape measure:
Use a steel tape measure to mark out surfaces for stoneblocking and for Grisaille. It is also useful for assessing the size of surfaces and therefore the quantity of paint or glaze you will require.

Straight edge:
Use a metal straight edge for marking outlines prior to decorating. Wooden straight edges are less satisfactory as they can be prone to warping, and are more easily damaged by sharp craft knives or scalpels.

Tracing paper:
Use semi-transparent tracing paper to copy the outlines of patterns and motifs from source material such as books or prints in order to transfer them to oiled-card when stencilling (see pages 44-5).

Triangle:
A set-square (or triangle) is a useful tool for checking true right-angles when marking-up for stoneblocking or for dividing a frame into sections when creating a tortoiseshell effect.

Wet-and-dry paper:
Use wet-and-dry paper, otherwise known as silicone carbide paper, to both smooth and key eggshell groundcoats prior to subsequent application of paints or glazes. You should use it with water in order to minimize both the creation of dust and the risk of scratching the surface (sometimes a problem with sandpaper).

Coarse- and medium-grades of wet-and-dry are best for keying, while fine grades are best for smoothing down (eg. on satin- or gloss-varnished surfaces prior to waxing and polishing).

Materials

PAINTS AND PIGMENTS

Artist's acrylics:
Solvent in water, artist's acrylics are available in tube form in a wide variety of colours. You will find them most useful for tinting white (latex) emulsion glazes and washes to the required colour (see Mixing water-based glazes). They can also be simply thinned with water to produce translucent glazes and washes in their own right, and they are waterproof when dry. Because of their fast drying times they are useful for applying rapid overlays of colour. However, the drawback is that you will have little or no time to distress the glaze or wash before it dries.

Artist's gouache:
Like artist's acrylics, you can use artist's gouache pigments to tint latex (emulsion) glazes and washes to the required colour, and thin them with water to produce glazes in their own right. Although they are less dense and hard-wearing than acrylics, gouache pigments lend washes and glazes a delicate, brushy texture not quite matched by acrylic formulations. However, they are not waterproof when dry.

Artist's oil paints:
These oil-based paints, consisting of pigment and linseed oil, are available in tube form in a wide range of colours. Mix them with transparent oil glaze and mineral spirits (white spirit) to create translucent glazes (see Mixing oil-based glazes). Unlike glazes mixed by thinning eggshell paint with white spirit, they need to be protected from wear and tear with one or two coats of varnish. You can also use them to tint opaque oil-based paints (undercoats, flat-oils and eggshells) to the required colour.

Eggshell paint:
This mid-sheen finish paint is available in a wide variety of pre-mixed colours. Use it primarily for creating smooth, non-porous groundcoats (which are ideal) for translucent glazes.
You can also tint white eggshell to the desired colour with artist's oil paints and universal stainers, and you can use coloured eggshells as a cheaper and harder-wearing substitute for artist's oils when tinting oil-based glazes.

Egg tempera:
Water-based egg tempera paint is available in tube form in a variety of colours. It dries to a hard-wearing, washable finish, and is particularly suitable for freehand painting and mural work.

Flat-oil paint:
You can use matte-finish, flat-oil paint, tinted with artist's oils to the desired colour, over primed and undercoated surfaces to provide a "ready keyed" opaque ground coat for translucent glazes. However, because they are more absorbent and less hardwearing, they are less suitable for this purpose than oil-based eggshell.

Latex (emulsion) paints:
Water-based latex (emulsion) paints are available pre-mixed in white and a wide variety of colours, and opaque matte and mid-sheen (satin) finishes. You can thin them with water and clear latex (emulsion) glaze (water-based varnish) to make glazes and washes, and tint white latex (emulsion) with artist's acrylics or gouache or universal stainers to the required colour.
However, latex (emulsion) paints do have certain limitations as far as specialist decorating is concerned. First, when they are used as an opaque groundcoat for super-imposed glazes they present a rougher surface (which is unsuitable for smoothing with wet-and-dry paper) than oil-based eggshell paint. This applies to silk-finish latex (emulsion) paints as well as the matte variety, albeit less so.
Second, they are more porous than an eggshell groundcoat and thus make any superimposed glaze dry much faster. This leaves you with less time to distress the glaze.
Third, and similarly, a latex (emulsion) glaze or wash dries much faster than an oil-based glaze. Again, this leaves you with less time to work it. (Of course, this isn't a problem with colourwashing – see page 62 – when you are deliberately trying to create a spontanaeous-looking, brushy effect.)
Fourth, if applied over bare wood they may raise the grain, and fifth, if applied over bare metal they will in time induce rust.

Metallic paints:
These opaque oil-based paints are available in various metallic colours, notably gold, bronze and silver. You can use them as pre-mixed basecoats for metallic finishes such as a Verdigris effect.

Powder colours:
Finely ground powder pigments (also available in liquid form) are solvent in water, relatively inexpensive, and available in a wide variety of natural or chemically manufactured colours. You can use them when mixing your own paints for colourwashing (see the instructions for mixing water-based glazes and washes), as well as for tinting proprietary water- and oil-based paints, glazes and varnishes. Some powder colours are toxic, so you should take precautions to protect your eyes, lungs and skin.

Primers:
Oil-based primers, solvent in mineral spirits (white spirit) are available in different formulations for sealing wood, bare plaster and various metals prior to under-coating.
You can also purchase an acrylic primer/undercoat for sealing bare wood. It is solvent in water and has a rapid drying time (1-2 hours). Where time is of the essence, use it as a substitute for slower-drying traditional oil-based primers and undercoats. However, you should note that, being water-based acrylic primer/undercoat may well slightly raise the grain of the underlying wood (which would then require re-sanding). It can also be used to prime canvas.
If you apply an undercoat or a latex (emulsion) paint over a previously painted surface and any underlying (unstable) pigment starts to "bleed" through into the new coat (this is often the case with reds, which are particularly unstable), you will have to apply one or two coats of aluminium primer, in accordance with the manufacturer's instructions, before proceeding to paint the surface.

Undercoat:
This opaque matte finish paint is available in white and a limited range of colours. Use one or two coats over a primed surface to provide a "ready keyed" finish for eggshell or flat-oil groundcoats. You can also use undercoat as an inexpensive substitute for white artist's oil when mixing oil-based glazes.

Universal stainers:
These chemical dyes are available in tube form in a limited range of colours, and are solvent in mineral spirits (white spirit). You can use them to tint both latex (emulsion) and oil-based paints and glazes. While they are less costly than artist's oils, the colours are "cruder" and very intense, and need to be heavily diluted and carefully mixed.

MEDIUMS AND SOLVENTS

Denatured alcohol (methylated spirits):
Use denatured alcohol to dilute shellac and distress wet or dry water-based latex (emulsions). By spattering it on you will create a localized cissing reaction in the paint that gives the appearance of certain types of marble or stone-work. By sponging or ragging it on you can produce a mottled finish, aesthetically pleasing in its own right and a simulation of the breakdown of pigments that occurs naturally over time in many traditional paints.

Linseed oil:
This pale yellow liquid is an ingredient of transparent oil glaze (scumble glaze) and oil-based paints. Use boiled linseed oil, together with mineral spirits (white spirit, or turpentine substitute) to seal manila paper stencils before cutting out and applying paint and glazes.

Mineral spirits (white spirit):
Also known as turpentine substitute, mineral spirits (white spirit) are primarily used for diluting oil-based paints and varnishes and for cleaning brushes. However, you can also use them to distress wet oil-based paints and glazes in much the same way as denatured alcohol can be used on wet or dry water-based paints and glazes.

Transparent oil glaze:
Also known as scumble glaze, transparent oil glaze is a white or honey-coloured liquid that becomes colourless when thinned with mineral spirits (white spirit) and brushed out over a surface. Tint it with artist's oils, universal stainers or oil-based paints, thinned with mineral spirits, to produce translucent oil-based glazes (*see* Mixing glazes).

Vinegar (acetic acid):
You can use vinegar to produce a localized cissing action in water-based glazes, as in the technique for Bird's eye maple graining.

Water:
Use water, the least expensive of all solvents, in order to dilute water-based paints and water-soluble pigments when mixing washes and glazes.

White glue (PVA):
Use white glue neat to stick paper to surfaces when creating a Print Room (see pages 160-1); diluted with water to seal bare plaster prior to painting or papering; as a binding agent when mixing your own water-based paints and glazes and as a protective varnish. PVA white glue is not waterproof, while EVA white glue is.

MIXING OIL-BASED GLAZES

To create many of the decorative finishes and effects illustrated throughout the book, you will need to mix oil-based glazes. The glazes are made up of pigment(s) suspended in a clear medium and sufficiently thinned with a solvent to make them semi-transparent when applied over an opaque groundcoat. The tinted, semi-transparent glaze allows the underlying ground colour to "ghost" through it, thereby creating subtle combinations, depths and gradations of colour. The recipe for each glaze gives the approximate proportions of each pigment in relation to any other pigments included; the approximate proportions of solvent in relation to the clear medium; and the approximate proportions of combined pigments in relation to combined solvent and medium. For example, in glaze B for Ragging (see pages 64-5) the pigment consists of 6 parts burnt sienna artist's oil in proportion to 1 part alizarin crimson artist's oil. The medium consists of 3 parts transparent oil glaze in proportion to 2 parts mineral spirits (white spirit). When mixed together the proportion (or ratio) of combined pigments to medium equals 1 part pigments to 8 parts medium.

The actual quantity of glaze you require depends upon the absorbancy of the underlying surface and how thickly you apply the glaze. Consequently, it is virtually impossible to prescribe exact quantities. However, a useful rule of thumb is 1 litre (1/4 gallon) of glaze to cover approximately 30 square metres (33 square yards) of wall.

So, for example, to mix approximately 1 litre (1/4 gallon) of glaze B for Ragging you should:

1 Using an old artist's fitch to blend them thoroughly, mix 3/5ths of a litre of transparent oil glaze with 2/5ths of a litre of mineral spirits (white spirit). In other words, mix them in a ratio of 3:2. Do this in either a 2 litre (gallon) paint kettle or plastic bucket.
2 Squeeze the artist's oils from their tubes into another container. The total volume of pigment (artist's oils) should be approximately 1/9th of the volume of medium in the other container, and should consist of approximately 6/7ths burnt sienna and 1/7th alizarin crimson. In other words, the pigments (artist's oils) are mixed together in a ratio of 6 parts burnt sienna to 1 part alizarin crimson.
3 Pour a little of the blended clear medium into a third container and, again using an old artist's fitch, slowly blend in the pigment (artist's oils). You will end up with a coloured, cream-like liquid that should match the the relevant colour swatch shown against the recipe for the glaze (see page 65). At this stage don't worry about the translucency of the glaze – just the colour match. Add more pigment(s) if required.
4 Again using an old artist's fitch, gradually stir the coloured creamy liquid into the bulk of the clear medium contained in the first container. From time to time swatch a little of the colour over the terracotta eggshell groundcoat to test the translucency of the glaze. Add more medium to increase the translucency and more pigment(s) to increase the opacity, but in each case make sure you thoroughly blend the mixture.

The oil-based glaze described above contains artist's oils and transparent oil glaze. However, you can also mix an oil-based glaze by using flat-oil or eggshell paint, either pre-mixed or tinted to the required colour with artist's oils or universal stainers, and thinned to the required degree of translucency by thinning with mineral spirits (white spirits). Similarly, you can substitute oil-based or polyurethane varnish, tinted to the required colour, for the transparent oil glaze. In each case, the basic method of mixing is the same as for the Ragging glaze above.

MIXING WATER-BASED GLAZES AND WASHES

Latex (emulsion) paints can obviously be bought pre-mixed in the required colour and then simply thinned with water to the required degree of transparency. For example, a ratio of approximately 1 part paint to between 8 and 20 parts water will give you an effective mixture for colourwashing. Similarly, you can tint white latex (emulsion) paint with artist's acrylic or gouache, universal stainers or powder colours to the required colour, and then dilute with water to the required degree of translucency.

Alternatively, you can make a simple water-based glaze with just powder colours and water (although this will have to be varnished for protection after application). For example, to mix glaze D for Mahogany graining (see page 99):

1 Mix 1 part Van Dyke brown powder colour with 1 part black powder colour (ie. equal quantities of each), adding a little water until you have a coloured liquid with the consistency of cream.
2 Then gradually mix approximately three times the volume of water (ie. a ratio of 1 part pigment to 3 parts water) to produce the glaze. You can also add a small quantity of white glue (PVA) to the mix as a binding agent if a slightly harder-wearing finish is required.

As with oil-based glazes, the precise quantity of wash required for any particular job depends on how thinly you apply it, as well as the absorbency of the underlying surface. However, a very rough rule of thumb is 1 litre of latex (emulsion) or powder colour wash for every 30 square metres (33 square yards).

Traditional water-based washes, such as distemper and limewash, are slightly more complicated to mix than the washes above. But results make the extra effort worthwhile.

167

Materials, equipment and techniques

Distemper:

Distemper is available pre-mixed from various specialist suppliers (see the Directory, pages 172-5). However, because distemper only keeps for two or three days at most, you may wish to mix up your own on site. The quantities given are approximate, and are intended to provide coverage for the walls of an average-size room (60 square metres or 67 square yards):

1 Pour 5 litres (1 gallon) of cold water into a bucket with a capacity of at least 10 litres (2 gallons).

2 Slowly pour approximately 10 kilos (22lbs) of ground chalk (whiting) into the water so that it rises to a peak of approximately 10cms (4ins) above the top of the water. Then leave the whiting to soak overnight in the bucket.

3 Pour off approximately the top 5cms (2ins) of clear water from the top of the bucket the following morning.

4 In a separate container, dissolve some powder pigment (in the desired colour) in cold water, and slowly and thoroughly stir it into the ground chalk (whiting) and water mixture until you have achieved the desired colour.

5 Having made up a batch of animal glue size to a volume of approximately 10 per cent of that of the whiting and water, slowly stir the warm glue into the coloured ground chalk (whiting) and water until the mixture is the consistency of paint. You should make the glue size using the method outlined in steps 1-4 under Gesso. Also, you should ensure that the animal glue granules you buy contain alum, as this will inhibit mould growth in the distemper once it has been applied.

6 If the distemper begins to stiffen as it cools, you can overcome the problem by standing the container in a bath of hot water.

7 Apply the distemper as it is to provide an opaque groundcoat.

8 To use the distemper for colourwashing, you should thin it with water until it takes on the consistency of milk.

9 Finally, you must use the distemper within a couple of days of mixing it. After that it will start to go off, and therefore become unusable.

Limewash:

Limewash is an essential protective and decorative finish for walls that need to "breathe" – in other words, those made from traditional materials such as wattle and daub and cob and covered with lime renders and plasters. It can also be applied over modern plasters. However, it is unsuitable for impervious surfaces, such as portland cement renders, modern brick, flint and modern synthetic paints, which provide insufficient suction for the limewash to key to them. Consequently, if you are considering using limewash, you should always seek the advice of an architect or consultant who specializes in conservation work before proceeding.

Traditionally, limewash was made up from scratch on site. This involved first slaking lump lime in water to produce lime putty. However, this was a very dangerous process, since the highly caustic mixture boils fiercely and can easily splash into the eyes or onto the skin. Slaking lime also exposed the painter to toxic fumes that damaged the lungs. Consequently, if you intend to mix your own limewash, it is strongly recommended that you avoid this stage and purchase ready-made lime putty directly from one of the suppliers listed in the Directory. Almost all suppliers, as well as conservation groups like bodies like The Society for the Protection of Ancient Buildings, (see the Directory) provide fact sheets that give detailed advice on the preparation and application of limewash. Again, for successful results, and your own safety, you are strongly advised to carefully follow their instructions, in addition to the brief outline of how to prepare and apply limewash provided below.

Some suppliers will provide mature lime putty pre-mixed with pigment and raw linseed oil (a waterproofing agent for exterior applications of limewash). However, because the lime putty in this form has to be used within a few days of receiving it (it goes off rapidly), you may prefer to add the linseed and pigments yourself.

When mixing limewash you will need approximately 1 litre (1/5th gallon) of limewash for 3-6 square metres of wall, depending on the porosity and texture of the underlying surface. And you should allow for an application of three coats internally and four to five coats externally. Approximately 1 litre (1/5th gallon) of mature lime putty will make approximately 10 litres (2 gallons) of limewash.

When assessing quantities, make sure you mix up sufficient limewash for the job in one batch. You can almost guarantee that you will be unable to colour-match any subsequent batch to the first one. Also allow approximately 1/10th litre (1/6th pint) of raw linseed oil for every 10 litres (2 gallons) of limewash.

You should proceed as follows, bearing in mind that you should never apply limewash on rainy days, during a frost or if it is below freezing:

1 Using a stiff-bristled brush, wipe down the surface to remove dust, and treat any mould with a fungicide in accordance with the manufacturer's instructions. Also repair any damaged plaster with lime mortar and fine sand.

2 Keep plenty of clean water to hand for immediately washing off any splashes of limewash that accidently come into contact with your skin during mixing or application, and wear protective gloves and goggles at all times.

3 Dilute the powder pigment(s) with water to the desired colour in a metal container.

4 Gradually blend the lime putty with water in a large metal container until it is the consistency of smooth paste, and thoroughly stir in the linseed oil.

5 Gradually stir in more water until the mixture is the consistency of thin cream.

6 Sieve the mixture into another container, breaking down and/or removing any lumps as you do so.

7 Stir in the pre-diluted pigment until you have achieved the desired colour. But bear in mind that coloured limewash always looks darker when wet, and lighter when dry (for an example see page 34).

8 Gradually blend in more water until the mixture is the consistency of milk. It is now ready to apply.

9 Prepare the surface by spraying it with water. If it is too dry the limewash will gradually crack and become friable.

10 Apply the first thin coat of limewash with a large soft-bristled brush. Don't apply too thick a coat or it will show brush marks and be liable to crazing later on.

11 When the first coat has dried, lightly wet the wall again and then apply the second thin coat.

12 Repeat steps 10-11, applying a minimum of three coats internally and four or five externally, until you have achieved an opaque, silky-smooth finish.

13 Allow the surface to dry as slowly as possible, and if necessary protect it from rain, sun and wind by erecting a temporary screen. Provided that the limewash coats have been applied properly, a limewash finish will continue to strengthen and harden for several weeks after it has dried.

VARNISHES

Cellulose:

Clear cellulose sealants are available in one or two-pack formulations. You can apply them in one or two coats to provide a transparent, hardwearing and washable finish for bare wooden surfaces (for example, floors and table tops that are likely to be subject to excessive wear and tear. However, because these sealants give off toxic fumes during application, you must ensure adequate ventilation and are advised to wear a respiratory mask as a precaution.

Crackle varnish:

Use crackle varnish to simulate the fine cracks and crazing (craquelure) found on ageing ceramics and varnished and lacquered surfaces. You should always follow the manufacturer's instructions very carefully during application.

Goldsize:

Use oil- or Japan goldsize (the latter dries quicker) as an adhesive for transfer metal leaf and metallic powders when gilding, and for sealing metallic powders and gold paint. You can also tint the size with artist's oils.

Knotting compound:

Use this shellac-based liquid to seal the resinous knots in bare wood before painting or varnishing.

Oil-based varnish:

Traditional oil-based varnishes are available in matte, satin (mid-sheen) and gloss formulations. While they enrich underlying colours and provide fairly good protection against moisture and wear and tear, they have a tendency to yellow with age, particularly in poorly lit areas. They also dry very slowly, and are thus very susceptible to picking up dust from the atmosphere. However, by thinning them with a small quantity of white (mineral) spirits you will speed up the drying time. You can also tint them with artist's oils or universal stainers.

Polyurethane varnish:
Like traditional oil-based varnishes, polyurethane varnishes are available in matte, satin (mid-sheen) and gloss formulations. They are, however, slightly easier to apply and offer particularly effective protection against moisture, wear and tear, heat and alcohol. They also enrich underlying colours and have a tendency to yellow with age, although in the case of the latter, manufacturers are gradually overcoming the "problem".

Sanding sealer:
The main constituent of sanding sealer is shellac (see below). Use it to seal bare wood before varnishing.

Shellac:
Made from an insect secretion, shellac is available in a variety of grades (from standard brown to fine-grade orange shellac, otherwise known as button polish). Having thinned it with denatured alcohol (methylated spirits) you can use it as a quick-drying varnish for wooden surfaces.
You should use bleached shellac (white polish) for French polishing pale woods and for sealing knots in wood prior to the application of pale-coloured paints and glazes (see knotting compound). And use French enamel varnish, made from bleached and chemically dyed shellac and available in a variety of colours, to stain and varnish wood in one application.

Water-based varnish:
You can mix a simple water-based varnish by diluting white glue (PVA or EVA) with water. However, water-based varnishes, known as latex (emulsion) glazes, are also available pre-mixed in matte, satin (mid-sheen) and gloss formulations. Although a milky colour in the container, they brush out and dry transparent, and you can apply them over both water- and oil-based paints and glazes (albeit over the latter only in accordance with the manufacturer's instructions). Unlike oil-based or polyurethane varnishes, water-based varnishes have a fast drying time, which minimizes the risk of picking up dust from the atmosphere, and they do not yellow with age. However, they offer far less protection against moisture and general wear and tear, so whether you use them partly depends upon the location of the decorative finish in question.

Tips for successful varnishing:
Make sure that the underlying surface is completely dry and free from dust. Ensure that all adjacent areas are as dust-free as possible. Minimize draughts from nearby doors and windows. Don't wear items of clothing (such as woollen pullovers) that are prone to shedding fibres. Avoid working in a damp atmosphere – excessive moisture will produce a milky white bloom in some varnishes as they dry. Always use a varnishing brush (*see* Brushes, page 164). Keep a wet edge going as you work. Finally, always follow the manufacturer's instructions, particularly with regard to diluting the varnish and the recommended drying times between coats.

WOOD STAINS

Wood stains come in a variety of formulations (see below). For more information, refer to the chapter on Staining, Waxing and Liming. Bear in mind that whatever type of stain you use, the original colour of the underlying wood will effect the colour of the stain. For example, a mahogany stain will turn pale beech mid-brown, while turning oak a dark brown. Many wood stains are highly toxic, so you must always protect eyes, hands and lungs when using them.

Water-based stains:
Make water-based stains for wood by mixing powder colours (for example, Van Dyke brown and black) with water. The more pigment you use, the darker the resulting stain. The drawback to using water-based stains is that they may raise the grain of the wood (which would then need re-sanding).

Chemical stains:
Chemicals such as blue copperas, biochromate of potash and copper sulphate can be mixed with water to stain wood. They work by reacting with the tannic acid in the wood to produce changes in colour. However, the change in colour can be unpredictable, and depends on the levels of tannic acid present. Blue copperas, for example, tends to turn all woods various shades of gray. On the other hand, biochromate of potash will turn beech a light tan colour, oak a greenish brown and walnut a pale yellow hue.

Oil-based stains:
Proprietary oil-based wood stains are available in a variety of colours. They tend to produce stronger colours than other stains, and have the considerable advantage over water-based stains of not raising the grain of the wood.

Spirit-based stains:
Mix spirit-based wood stains by dissolving powder colours in denatured alcohol (methylated spirits) and then mixing in French polish as a binder, in a ratio of approximately 1 part French polish to 4 parts denatured alcohol. The main disadvantage of spirit-based stains is that they tend to fade quite noticably over time.

Bleaches:
You can use oxalic acid to lighten the colour of wood. However, it is highly poisonous, so great care should be taken when handling it, and the wood should be washed down with acetic acid and water to remove any residue of the acid afterward.

SUNDRY MATERIALS

Gesso:
Made from ground chalk (whiting) and rabbit-skin glue, gesso has been used for thousands of years on joinery, furniture and other wooden artefacts to conceal crudely made joints, fill in the grain and provide a silky-smooth and resilient ground for decoration, particularly gilding and marbling. Nowadays, pre-mixed synthetic gesso is available from specialist decorating suppliers, and can be applied straight from the tin (for application, *see* Preparing surfaces, page170). However, you may wish to mix it yourself, using the following method:
1 Soak rabbit-skin glue granules in water overnight until they are soft – in a ratio of 1 part granules to 8 parts water.
2 Fill the bottom container of a bain marie with water, and place the glue granules and water in the top container. Heat gently (do not boil) until the granules have completely dissolved.
3 Remove the mixture from the heat, and strain it into a container through a nylon stocking. Then leave it to cool off and coagulate. It should set to the consistency of jelly. If it breaks up when you push a stick or your fingers into it, the mixture is too "strong", and will

flake off when applied to the wood. In which case, add a little water and repeat steps 2-3 again. Similarly, if the mixture is too weak or sloppy, it will crumble and powder when applied. To remedy this, add more glue granules and repeat steps 1-3.
4 Put the jelly back into the top container of the bain marie and gently re-heat until it dissolves. Then sieve in the ground chalk (whiting), stirring gently with a wooden stick or spoon until the mixture has the consistency of pre-mixed paint. Make sure that the mixture doesn't come to the boil.
5 Using a wooden spoon, push the mixture through a fine sieve four or five times to make sure that it has been properly mixed. And finally, add two or three drops of linseed oil to stop the gesso cracking when it is applied to the surface.
6 If you are not going to use the gesso immediately, pour it into an airtight jar and refrigerate to stop it going mouldy.
(Again, for the appropriate method of application *see* Preparation of surfaces, pages 170-1).

Metal patinating fluids:
Chemical patinating fluids are available from specialist suppliers in a variety of formulations for rapidly "ageing" different types of metal, such as steel, bronze, brass, silver and gold. Because such fluids are highly corrosive, you must protect your eyes, skin and lungs when handling them. It is also essential that you always follow the manufacturer's instructions with regard to application very carefully. You will also need to apply a fixing agent to stabilize the patinating fluid once it has "aged" the metal to the required degree.

Metallic powders:
Use fine metallic powders, available from suppliers of artist's materials in a range of colours, such as gold, bronze and silver, for powder gilding. You can also mix metal powders with white glue (PVA) or varnish in order to produce metallic paints.

Paint and varnish strippers:
Use proprietary chemical strippers to remove old layers of paint and varnish from wooden (and metal) surfaces prior to redecorating. Because they are highly caustic and give off noxious vapours, you must protect your eyes, hands and lungs when using them.

Plaster:
Use white or pink gypsum finishing plaster, available from builder's merchants and do-it-yourself stores, for creating a distressed plaster finish (see pages 42-3). Unlike plaster of Paris, finishing plaster dries reasonably slowly, which allows you more time to smooth it down with a plasterer's float or trowel before it sets.

Rottenstone:
Mix rottenstone, a fine, gray-coloured limestone powder, with a little lemon oil to form a mildly abrasive paste for polishing varnished surfaces (for example, to give *faux* marble effects a deep, lustrous finish see marbling, pages 110-114). You can also use it mixed with beeswax polish and a little turpentine to create an antiquing glaze.

Stencils
Card stencils are printed on manila paper, and must be sealed with a mixture of equal parts boiled linseed oil and white spirit, and left to dry before cutting out. Acetate stencils are easier to use if the pattern or motif is applied in two or three stages.
You can, of course, cut your own stencils (*see* Stencilling, pages 54-5).

Transfer metal leaf:
Booklets of gold and silver transfer metal leaf on wax paper backing sheets are available from suppliers of artist's materials. You can also use transfer Dutch metal leaf, again available in booklet form, as an effective and less expensive substitute for gold and silver leaf. This product is available in a number of metal effects, including copper and bronze.

Waxes:
Proprietary antiquing waxes for protecting and "ageing" wood are available from specialist suppliers. However, you can make your own by mixing beeswax polish with a little turpentine and either rottenstone or powder colours. Professional decorators sometimes use shoe polish, in various shades of brown, as an inexpensive and effective substitute. Liming waxes are also available but, again, you can make your own by:
1 Gently heating beeswax in a bain marie until it becomes liquid.
2 Mixing in titanium white powder colour (in a ratio of approximately 1 part powder to 3 parts beeswax).
3 Pouring the mixture into a separate container and then allowing it to set.
Liming waxes are appropriate for open-grained woods (and for antiquing bare plaster), but you should use liming paste on closer-grained woods and exposed surfaces likely to be subject to wear and tear and thus requiring varnishing.
Again, liming pastes are commercially available, but you can make your own by:
1 Mixing approximately 1 tablespoon of titanium powder colour with 1 pint (600 ml) of water to the consistency of single cream.
2 Adding roughly 8 tablespoons of rabbit skin glue that has been gently heated in a bain marie.

Whiting (ground chalk):
Use whiting, a fine-ground chalk free from impurities, to add body and texture to water-based glazes and washes such as Distemper. You can also use it over eggshell basecoats before graining with water-based glazes.

Preparing surfaces

Bare Plaster:
You will need a smooth, firm and unblemished surface to carry out your decorative finish on, so unless they are to be included as part of the decorative finish, you should scrape out patches of loose ("live") plaster with a steel spatula. Then chamfer the edges of the holes with coarse- or medium-grade sandpaper, and dust down the surface. Next dampen the holes (and adjacent areas) with a little water. Then fill them with a commercially available spackle (filler), in accordance with the manufacturer's instructions, to a level that is just higher than, and slightly overlapping the surrounding surface.
Once the filler has thoroughly dried out, level the repair by rubbing down with medium-and fine-grade sandpapers. Finally, repair shallow cracks and other minor imperfections with a fine-grade spackle (filler), and when dry smooth down with fine-grade sandpaper.
To prepare the plaster for a decorative finish employing modern latex (emulsion) water-based paints and glazes, prime it with a thin wash of white or suitably coloured matte latex (emulsion) paint.
When dry, apply one or two opaque coats of matte or silk (mid-sheen) latex (emulsion) paint in the colour specified for the basecoat of the finish in question.
Note: Prior to an application of traditional water-based limewash or distemper over modern or traditional plasters and renders, use the preparatory techniques outlined under Limewash, *see* page 167.
To prepare the plaster for a decorative finish employing oil-based paints and glazes, first seal the surface with oil-based primer. Once this has dried, apply a minimum of one coat of an opaque oil-based undercoat in either white or an appropriate colour. Finally, apply one or two coats of eggshell paint in the colour specified for the basecoat of the finish or effect.

Painted plaster:
If the painted surface is sound, wash it down with warm soapy water and a little disinfectant, rinse with clean water and allow to dry. Treat mould with a commercial fungicide. If the paint is oil-based gloss or eggshell, key the surface by rubbing down with coarse- or medium-grade wet-and-dry paper.
If the decorative finish is to be executed in oil-based paints and glazes, apply one or two oil-based undercoats in an appropriate colour prior to the application of one or two coats of the specified eggshell oil-based basecoat.
If the finish employs water-based latex (emulsion) paints and glazes, apply them in one or two matte or silk coats directly on top of the cleaned and keyed surface. Note that the pigments used in some paints can be unstable – reds are often a problem – and have a tendency to bleed through undercoat or latex (emulsion) paint. If you are faced with this problem you will need to apply one or two coats of a aluminium primer after cleaning and keying the surface. If the paint is unsound – for example, if its seems to be bubbling or flaking – clean it as above and then rub it down with a medium-grade sandpaper before applying a surface sealer. Then level out any surface irregularities with spackle (fine grade surface filler), smooth down with fine-grade sand- or wet-and-dry paper, and re-seal before applying undercoat or latex (emulsion) paint as above.
Finally, if the bubbling or flaking is particularly bad it is often better to clean, rub down and seal the surface as above, and then cover it with lining paper before applying paint.

Wallpaper:
Strip off damaged or peeling wallpaper and repair and prepare the underlying bare plaster before painting or re-papering.
Provided it is in good condition, previously painted paper should be wiped down with warm soapy water and disinfectant, rinsed and, when dry, prepared as for painted plaster. However, you should note that most vinyl papers will not take a latex (emulsion) basecoat, and must be sealed with an oil-based undercoat.

Concrete floors:
To level off or repair concrete floors for *faux* marble or stone finishes, apply a commercially available, self-levelling screed. Repair any small holes and cracks with spackle (filler) and smooth down as for bare plaster. Two coats of linoleum paint will provide a smooth, hard-wearing and non-porous ground for the decorative finish. Because of problems with keying the surface, vinyl flooring is an unsatisfactory base for paint finishes.)

Unglazed pottery and earthenware:
Before applying the specified

basecoat, seal terracotta with one or two coats of white glue (PVA) diluted with a little water.

Ceramics:
Because of the difficulty in keying the smooth, hard surface, ceramic tiles and the like present a similar problem to that posed by vinyl flooring. However, ceramic sealants are available from some decorating outlets and should be applied prior to decoration, in accordance with the manufacturer's instructions.

Glass:
Wash the surface down with soapy water to remove grease, dirt and dust, rinse with clean water and then allow to dry. Next, roughen the surface with coarse- or medium-grade wet-and-dry paper. Finally, apply up to three coats of oil-based undercoat, prior to brushing on one or two oil-based eggshell basecoats in the appropriate colour.

Metal surfaces:
To remove paint from metal surfaces prior to re-painting or applying a metal patinating fluid open windows and doors to ensure adequate ventilation and allow noxious fumes to escape.
Next, put on goggles, a face mask and chemical-resistant gloves to protect your eyes, lungs and hands. Then brush on several coats of commercial spirit-based paint stripper and, as the paint begins to blister, rub it off with a wire brush and a coarse-grade steel (wire) wool. Once all the paint has been removed, neutralize any residue of stripper left on the surface by rubbing down with a rag soaked in mineral spirits (white spirit).
If the metal surface is to be given a paint finish, rather than chemically patinated, treat any evident rust by brushing on a commercial rust inhibitor. Then apply one or two coats of metal primer and, once dry, apply one or two coats of oil-based undercoat. Finally, apply the flat-oil or eggshell basecoats specified for the decorative finish.

Laminated particleboard (chipboard):
Wash down laminated surfaces with soapy water to remove grease, dirt and dust. Then rinse thoroughly with clean water and allow to dry. To key the surface either rub it down vigorously with coarse-grade wet-and-dry paper or, if you can obtain it from a specialist supplier,

brush on a coat of laminate primer in accordance with the manufacturer's instructions. Finally, apply one or two coats of oil-based undercoat, prior to brushing on the specified basecoat.

Hardboard:
Before undercoating and applying a flat-oil or eggshell basecoat, bare hardboard should first be primed with hardboard sealant. Hardboard that has already been painted should be prepared in the same way as painted plaster (see page 170).

Waxed and oiled wood:
Prior to painting, wax and oil must be removed from wood by gently rubbing down the surface in the direction of the grain with mineral spirits (white spirit) and a light grade (00) steel (wire) wool. When the wax or oil begins to dissolve, continue the process using a clean, lint-free rag soaked in the spirits. Before applying paint, follow the instructions for preparation of bare wood. If you wish to create a very smooth surface for gilding or marbling, refer to the instructions for gesso on page 169.

Shellacked and varnished wood:
Providing the surface is in good condition, shellac and varnish can be cleaned and keyed for painting in the same way as painted wood. However, damaged shellac must be removed by rubbing down with denatured alcohol (methylated spirits) and light-grade (00) steel (wire) wool. Flaking cellulose can be removed with a commercial paint stripper, as outlined under the instructions for painted wood (below). Other types of varnish should be removed with commercial varnish stripper. For additional preparation, refer to the instructions for Bare Wood and Gesso (right).

Painted wood:
If you are applying a paint finish, sound painted wooden surfaces, or those exhibiting only minor damage, should be prepared using the same method outlined under painted plaster above.
Flaking, peeling or bubbling paint must, however, be removed. Begin by opening windows and doors to ensure adequate ventilation and allow the escape of noxious fumes. Put on goggles, a face mask and chemical-resistant rubber gloves to protect eyes, lungs and hands. Then brush on several coats of spirit-

based paint stripper (do not use a water-based stripper as it will raise the grain of the underlying wood). Scrape off the paint as it begins to bubble and blister with a metal scraper and 0 grade steel wool. Always work in the direction of the grain, and use a small wire brush to remove paint debris from the recesses of any mouldings. When all the paint has been removed, rub down the exposed wood with a rag soaked in mineral spirits (white spirit) in order to neutralize the residue of stripper left on the surface. Finally, to prepare the surface for painting, marbling or gilding you should refer to the instructions for Bare wood and Gesso.

Bare wood:
To prepare bare or untreated wood for a paint finish you must cover any exposed nail or screw heads with two coats of metal primer. Fill any holes or cracks with flexible wood spackle (filler), rubbing down when dry to create a smooth finish level with adjacent areas.
Cover exposed knots with two or three coats of white knotting compound if you are painting on top, and two or three coats of clear knotting compound if you are staining or varnishing. Once the knotting compound has dried, brush on a coat of oil-based wood primer, and again allow to dry. Finally, apply one or two coats of oil-based undercoat prior to the application of the specified eggshell basecoat.
Note: To create an especially smooth surface prior to gilding or marbling, you can use gesso instead of a proprietary modern spackle (filler). Pre-mixed gesso is available from suppliers of artist's materials, but you can also make your own (for method *see* page 169).
Apply gesso as follows:
1 Key the primed wooden surface by rubbing it down with coarse- or medium-grade sandpaper.
2 Fill any open or badly-fitting joints by soaking pieces of linen (or silk) in a thin solution of gesso and pressing them into the crevices.
3 Having smoothed down the gesso-soaked material with your finger or a flat piece of wood, leave to dry for a minimum of two days.
4 Keeping the gesso in the top container of a bain marie and leaving hot water in the bottom container to stop it setting during application, apply the first coat with a hog's hair brush, brushing out in

one direction only. When you have covered the entire surface, allow it to dry.
5 Apply the second coat of gesso in the same way, but brush it out at 90 degrees to the first one. Then repeat the process until you have built up seven or eight coats – each brushed out at 90 degrees to the previous coat, and each applied only after the previous coat has dried.
6 Once the final coat has dried, smooth down the surface with fine-grade steel (wire) wool. It is now ready for gilding, but if you wish to apply an oil-based paint – as you would do, for example, when marbling – first seal the gesso with a thin coat of shellac or matte varnish.

Directory

BRITAIN

PAINTS, PAPERS AND MATERIALS

Marthe Armitage
1 Strand on the Green
Chiswick
London W4 3PQ
Hand-painted and period-style wallpapers.

J.W. Bollom Group
PO Box 76
Croydon Road
Beckenham
Kent BR3 4BL
Manufacturers and suppliers of a wide range of paints, varnishes, stains, waxes and specialist decorating equipment.

C. Brewer
327 Putney Bridge Road
London SW15 2PG
Suppliers of a wide range of decorating materials and equipment.

Brodie and Middleton Ltd
68 Drury Lane
London WC2B 5SP
Suppliers of decorating brushes, metallic powders, paints, pigments and powder colours.

H.J. Chard and Son
Feeder Road
Bristol BS2 0JJ
Limewashes, plasters and renders.

Cole & Son Ltd
18 Mortimer Street
London W1A 4BU
Special period paints, including Georgian gray and Queen Anne white. Wallpapers, borders and fabrics.

Colefax and Fowler
39 Brook Street
London W1
Period-style wallpapers.

Cornelissen & Son Ltd
105 Great Russell Street
London WC1B 3RY
Specialists in period-style paints and powder pigments.

Craig and Rose plc
172 Leith Walk
Edinburgh EH6 5EP
Manufacturers and suppliers of traditional varnishes, including extra pale dead-flat varnish.

Crown Berger Europe Ltd
PO Box 37
Crown House
Hollins Road
Darwen
Lancashire BB3 0BG
Manufacturers of a wide range of interior and exterior paints.

Crown Decorative Products Ltd
PO Box 22
Queens Mill
Hollins Road
Lancashire
BB3 0BD
Suppliers of traditional wallpapers, including a range of Lincrusta papers.

Daler-Rowney Ltd
12 Percy Street
London W1A 2BP
Manufacturers and suppliers of a wide range of artist's materials.

The Design Archives
79 Walton Street
London SW3 2HP
Manufacturers of wallpapers reproduced from original 17th-, 18th- and 19th-century designs.

Elizabeth Eaton
30 Elizabeth Street
London SW1 9RB
Period-style papers, paint effects and painted furniture.

Mary Fox Linton
Unit 4s
Hewlett House
Haverlock Terrace
London
SW8 4AS
Period-style wallpapers.

Green & Stone
259 King's Road
London SW3 5EL
and
1 North House
North Street
Chichester
PO19 1HE
Suppliers of a wide range of specialist decorating materials, crackle varnish, stencils and transparent oil glaze.

Greenham Trading
Telford Place
Crawley
West Sussex
Suppliers of Solvex chemical-resistant gloves.

Charles Hammond Ltd
2a Battersea Park Road
London SW8 5BJ
Period Fabrics

Heart of the Country
Home Farm
Swinsen
Nr Litchfield
Staffordshire S14 9QR
Specialists in American period-style paints.

Karls
6 Cheval Place
London SW7 1EF
Suppliers to the trade of Swedish reproduction wallpapers.

John T Keep & Sons Ltd
15 Theobald's Road
London
WC1X 8FN
Suppliers of crackle varnish, transparent oil glaze and universal stains.

John Myland
80 Norwood High Street
London SE27 9NW
Suppliers of artist's brushes, liming wax, pigments, powder colours, rottenstone and transparent oil glaze.

National Trust
c/o Farrow and Ball (Southern) Ltd
Uddens Trading Estate
Wimborne
Dorset BH21 7NL
Period-style paints (57 colourways).

John Oliver Ltd
33 Pembridge Road
London W11 3HG

Osborne & Little plc
304 Kings Road
London
SW3 5UH
and
39 Queen Street
Edinburgh
EH2 3NH
Designers and manufacturers of furnishing fabrics, wallpapers and borders.

Paper Moon
Unit 2
Brent Trading Estate
390 North Circular Road
London NW10
Decorative wallpaper borders.

Papers and Paints
4 Park Walk
London SW10 0AD
Specialist paints and decorating materials, range of "historic" colours. Also colour-matching service.

E. Ploton (Sundries) Ltd
273 Archway Road
London N6 5AA
Wide range of paints, varnishes and decorating equipment, including gilding and crackle varnish.

Potmolen Paints
27 Woodstock Industrial Estate
Warminster
Wiltshire BA12 9DX
Conservation-grade limewashes, casein and oil-bound distemper, biodegradable stripper.

Putnams Painting & Designs Ltd
55 Regents Park Road
London NW1 8XD
Supplier of Mediterranean palette pigments and paints.

J.H. Ratcliffe & Co (Paints) Ltd
135a Linaker Road
Southport
Lancashire
Manufacturer of paints and varnishes.

The Rose of Jericho Ltd
PO Box 53
Kettering
Northamptonshire
NN14 3BN
Suppliers of a wide range of traditional paints and materials.

Arthur Sanderson and Sons
52 Berners Street
London W1P 3AD
Hand-printed wallpapers.

Simpsons Paints Ltd
122-4 Broadley Street
London NW8 8BB
Specialist brushes, gold leaf and transparent oil glaze.

Stuart R. Stevenson
68 Clerkenwell Road
London EC1M 5QA
Suppliers of artist's and gilding materials.

Top Layer Ltd
5 Egerton Terrace
London SW3 2BX
Wallpapers and fabrics from any period.

Toynbee-Clarke Interiors Ltd
95 Mount Street
London W1
Restoration and installation of antique wallpapers.

Warner Fabrics plc
7-11 Noel Street
London
W1V 4AL
Manufacturers and suppliers of traditional wallcoverings.

Watts & Co Ltd
7 Tufton Street
London
SW1P 3QE
Hoar Cross collection of handprinted Victorian Gothic wallcoverings.

Zimmer and Rhodes
103 Cleveland Street
London
W1P 5PL
Period-style wallpapers.

Zoffany Ltd
63 South Audley Street
London W1
Manufacturers of Document wallpapers, including handprinted Temple Newsam Coll.

PAINT ARTISTS AND INTERIOR DECORATORS

Jonathan Alexander Ltd
28 Connaught Street
London W2 2AF
Paint finishes, wood graining and period-style wallpapers.

Ambience (Construction) Ltd
81 Storforth Lane
Trading Estate
Hasland
Chesterfield
Derbyshire S42 6NU
Paint techniques and murals.

Richard Bagguley
18 Streathborne Road
London SW17 8QX
Specializes in paint finishes and trompe l'oeil.

Jacqueline Bateman
7 Rylett Crescent
London W12 9RP
Murals, trompe l'oeil, stencils, friezes and pastiche.

Guy Bedford
4 Goddards Green
Benenden
Cranbrook, Kent
Furniture decorator and restorer, jappaner (oriental lacquerwork) and murals.

R.H. Bennett
The Lime Centre
Long Barn
Morestead
Winchester
Hampshire SO21 1LZ
Runs one-day courses in limewashing.

Bennison
91 Pimlico Road
London SW1W 8PH
Interior design and decoration.

John Beveridge
52b Tollington Road
London N7 61G
Murals, faux finishes and all paint techniques.

Dorothy Boyer Interiors
Oakdene
Hurston Lane
Storrington
West Sussex
Murals, trompe l'oeil and all paint finishes.

Andrew Bradley
1 St Saviours Terrace
Larkhall
Bath
Decorative finishes, eg. marbling, stippling and rag-rolling.

Chance and Leese Associates
Brant Hill
Wells Next the Sea
Norfolk
Marbling and graining.

Jane Churchill Designs
81 Pimlico Road
London
SW1W 8PH
Interior design and decoration.

Colefax and Fowler
39 Brook Street
London
W1Y 1AU
Interior design and decoration.

George Cooper Ltd
26 Cale Street
London SW3 3QU
All specialist finishes, including marbling.

Leila Corbett Ltd
Alexandra Studios
3 Jubilee Place
London SW3 3TD
All specialist paint finishes.

The Country House Collection
The Tything
Preston Court
Ledbury
Herefordshire
HR6 2LL
Specializes in the Elizabethan period.

Marco Crivello
5 Tankerville Road
Streatham
London SW16 5LL
Decorative paint techniques eg. Renaissance, faux bois, faux marbre and murals.

DKT (Davies Keeling Trowbridge)
Unit 5
Charter House Works
Eltringham Street
London SW18 1TD
Decorative paint finishes.

Hannerle Dehn
The Studio Centre
Studio 7
Ranelagh Gardens
London SW7
Specializes in hand-painted fabrics and paint finishes.

Mark Done
3 Mount Fort Terrace
Barnsbury Square
London N1 1JJ
Decorator specializing in a wide range of finishes including woodgraining and tortoiseshelling.

Elizabeth Eaton
25a Basil Street
London SW3 1BB
Interior design and decoration.

Jon Edgson
38 Dyer Street
Cirencester
Gloucester Gl7 2PF
Paint finishes, gilding and wallpapers.

Lionel Fantom
The Officer's House
Rye Harbour
Sussex
Gilder, signwriter and paint techniques.

Fine Design
Fairholme Works
Jawbone Hill
Oughtibridge
Sheffield S30 3HN
All paint techniques, including murals, clouding and crackle glazing.

Christophe Gollut
116 Fulham Road
London SW3 6HU
Interior decorator specializing in continental-influenced interiors.

Gorlich Interiors
22 Ashford Road
Tenterden
Kent TN30 6QU
Interior designer.

Rosemary Hearn Interior Design
Westwell
Ashford
Kent TN25 4JP
Murals, stencilling, dragging and marbling.

Simon Hickman
32c Richmond Road
Staines, Middlesex
Paint finishes, murals and graining.

Lindsay Hiscox & Associates
7 Edith Grove
London SW10 0JZ
All paint finishes.

Helena Hood & Co
3 Margaret's Buildings
Brock Street
Bath, Avon
Interior design and decoration.

Jonathan Hudson
16 Fitzjames Avenue
London W14 0RP
Interior design and decoration.

Jocasta Innes
Paintability & House Style
Unit 3, Huguenot Place
17a Heneage Street
London E1 5LJ
Stencils, William Morris and ethnic designs, painted furniture, patterns and paint kits.

Sylvia Lawson Johnston Interior Design
35 Albert Street
Aberdeen AB1 1XU
Paint techniques.

Juliet Jowitt Wood House Design
Thorpe Lodge
Littlethorpe
Near Ripon
Yorkshire HG4 3LU
All paint techniques.

Catherine Lalau Keraly
104 Hereford Road
London W2 5AL
Art Deco, geometric approach to murals, sculptures and relief.

James Kerr and Alistair Erskine
153 Leathwaite Road
London SW11
Paint techniques, gessoing, stencilling and graining.

Jake Leith Partnership
12 Midland Road
Hemel Hempstead
Herts HP2 5BH
All paint finishes.

Ian Lieber
29 Craven Terrace
Lancaster Gate
London W2 3EL

Sara Jane Longlands
17 St Patrick's Road
South
Lytham St Annes
Lancashire FY8 1XP
Trompe l'oeil, screens and firescreens.

Kathryn Lyons Interiors Ltd
6 Pencombe Mews
Off Denbigh Road
London W11 2RZ
All paint techniques.

Sally Miles
37 Englewood Road
London SW12 9PA
Painted murals and trompe l'oeil.

Miller Partnership
Brownings Farm Craft Workshops
Blackboys, nr Uckfield
East Sussex TN22 5HG
All paint finishes.

Mrs Monro Ltd
11 Montpelier Street
London SW7
18th-century English country-house style.

Number Twelve Queen Street
Bath
Avon BA1 1NE
Interior design and decoration.

Anthony Paine Ltd
24 Highgate High Street
London N6 5JG
Interior design and decoration.

Pavilion Designs
49 Pavilion Road
London SW1X 0HD
Interior design and decoration.

Simon Playle Ltd
6 Fulham Park Studios
Fulham Park Road
London SW6 4LW
Interior design and decoration.

Private Lives
The Old Parsonage
Church Street
Crondall
Nr Farnham
Surrey GU10 5QQ
Interior design and decoration.

D.J. Reedman and T. Poole
7 Dickinson House
Turin Street
London E2
Specialist paint finishes, murals and trompe l'oeil.

Patrick Regan
c/o Tessuto Ltd
Chestnut House
Hall Street
Long Melford
Sudbury, Suffolk
Specializes in wood finishes, trompe l'oeil and all paint finishes.

P.M. Ruddell
26 rue de Colonel
Paris 15
France
Murals.

Directory

Schemes
56 Princedale Road
London W11 4NL
All paint techniques.

Jane Simcock Design Ltd
49 St Margaret's Grove
Twickenham
Middlesex TW1 1JF
Specialist paint finishes.

Sloane Decorators
4 Milner Street
London SW3 2PU
All paint finishes eg. glazing, graining, marbling and stencilling.

Smith and Cutts
45 Oxford Gardens
Chiswick
London W4
Decorative finishes, including trompe l'oeil and murals.

Society for the Preservation of Ancient Buildings (SPAB)
37 Spital Square
London E1 6DY
Information and advice on paint finishes eg. limewashing and distemper.

Sarah Stewart
Broken Colour
8 Coastguard Cottages
Rye Harbour
Rye, Sussex
All paint techniques and murals.

Stuart Interiors
Barrington Court
Barrington
Ilminster
Somerset TA19 0NQ
Recreates 16th- and 17th-century interiors.

Michael Synder
Trio Design
2 St Barnabas Street
London SW1W 8PE
Specialist decorator.

Henryk Terpilowski
22a Station Road
London NW10
Decorator, specializing in marbling, woodgraining and a wide range of finishes.

Tones
29 Streatley Road
London NW6 7LT
All paint techniques, including murals.

Jean Whitell
98 Forburg Road
London N16 6HT
Specializes in paint finishes.

Joanna Wood
Joanna Trading
7 Bunhouse Place
London SW1W 8HU
Interior design and decoration.

Wormell and Dilworth
174 Camden Road
London NW1 98J
Specialize in scenic painting and all paint techniques.

Melissa Wyndham
6 Sydney Street
London SW3
Interior design and decoration.

Robert Young
68 Battersea Bridge Road
London SW11 3AG
Distemper, lime washes and primitive wall decoration.

UNITED STATES

Absolute Coatings, Inc.
34 Industrial Street
Bronx NY 10461
Varnishes.

Adele Bishop
PO Box 3349
CL40
Kinston NC 28501
Stencils (old and new designs), paints, brushes, how-to-books. Mail order.

Art Essential of New York Ltd
3 Cross Street
Suffern NY 10801-4601
Distributor of gold leaf supplies.

Art Supply Warehouse
360 Main Avenue
(Route 7)
Norwalk CT 06851
Retail suppliers of artists' paints, brushes and general art supplies. Also mail order service.

Binney and Smith, Inc.
1100 Church Lane
PO Box 431
Easton PA 18044-0431
Publishers of Liquitex Color Maps and Mixing Guides.

Dick Blick Fine Art Company
PO Box 1267
Galesburg IL 61401
Artists' paints, brushes and general art supplies.

Bradbury & Bradbury Wallpapers
PO Box 155
Benicia CA 94510
Manufacturers and suppliers of wallpapers.

Brosse et Dupont
3 Milltown Court
Union
NJ 07083
Importer of a wide variety of brushes.

Central Art
1126 Walnut Street
Philadelphia
PA 19017
Artists' paints, brushes and general art supplies.

Chromatic Paint Corp.
PO Box 690
Stony Point NY 10980
Manufacturers of Japan colors.

Albert Constantine & Son, Inc.
2050 Eastchester Road
Bronx NY 10461
Paint strippers, brushes and varnishes.

Dover Publications
11 East Ninth Avenue
New York NY 10019
Suppliers of reference books, period paints and stencils by catalog and mail order.

Eagle Supply Company
327 West 42nd Street
New York NY 10036
Sign painters' supplies.

Finesse Pinstriping, Inc.
PO Box 1428
Linden Hill Station
Flushing NY 11354
Manufacturers of pinstriping tape.

Sam Flax, Inc.
39 West 19th Street
New York NY 10011
General art and graphic art supplies.

Frog Tool Company Ltd
700 West Jackson Boulevard
Chicago IL 60606
Paint strippers, brushes and varnishes.

Fuller-O'Brien Corp.
450 East Grand Avenue
South San Francisco
CA 84080

Gail Crisi Stencilling, Inc.
PO Box 1263
Haddonfield
New Jersey 08033
Pre-cut stencil designs (over 250 designs). Retail stores in New Jersey and mail order.

Grand Central Artists' Materials, Inc.
18 East 40th Street
New York NY 10016
General art and graphic art supplies.

Gail Grisi Stencilling, Inc.
405 Haddon Avenue
Haddonfield NJ 08033
Pre-cut stencils and paints.

Janovic Plasa's Incomplete Catalog
30-35 Thompson Avenue
Long Island City
NY 11101
Catalog of materials and equipment.

Koenig Artists' Supply Corp.
1777 Boston Post Road
Milford CT 06460
General art supplies.

Lee's Art Shop, Inc.
220 West 57th Street
New York NY 10019
General art supplies, including sea sponges and color mixing charts.

Lefranc & Bourgeois, Inc.
357 Cottage Street
PO Box 2484
Springfield
MA 01101 2484
Distributor of artists' paints and brushes.

Liberty Prints
Routes 66 and 23B
Hudson
NY 12534
Wide range of paints, glazes and brushes.

Long Island Paint Company
1 Continental Hill
Glen Cove
NY 11542
House and casein paints.

McCloskey Varnish Company
7600 State Road
Philadelphia
PA 19136
Ready-mixed glazes, flatting oil and varnishes.

Mohawk Finishing Products, Inc.
Route 30 North
Amsterdam NY 12010
and
1355 Chattahoochee Avenue NW
PO Box 20074
Howell Mill Station
Atlanta GA 30325
and
4653 Mint Way
Dallas TX 75236
and
1946 East Devon Avenue
Elk Grove Village
IL 60007
and
15622 Producer Lane
Huntingdon Beach
CA 92649
Suppliers of crackle lacquer and a range of polishes and shellacs.

Benjamin Moore & Company
51 Chestnut Ridge Road
Montvale
NJ 07645

National Trust
for Historical Preservation
1785 Massachusetts Ave, NW
Washington DC 20036

New York Central Art Supply
62 Third Avenue
New York NY 10003
General art supplies including spalter and brushes.

The Old Fashioned Milk Paint Company
Box 222
Groton MA 01450
Suppliers of milk paints.

Old House Journal
435 9th Street
Brooklyn NY 11215
Information on renovating, also sells gun and plate paint strippers.

Osborne and Little
979 Third Avenue
Suite 1503N
New York NY 10022
Traditional wallpapers and fabrics.

Pearl Paint
308 Canal Street
New York
NY10013
Suppliers of specialist brushes, art supplies and paints.

Plaid Enterprise
1849 International
Boulevard
Box 7600
Norcross
GA 30091
Suppliers of crackle lacquer.

Pottery Barn
100 North Point Street
San Francisco CA 94133
Amateur marbling kits.

Pratt & Lambert, Inc.
PO Box 22
Buffalo NY 14240
Paints, ready-mixed glazes and varnishes.

Renovator's Supply, Inc.
Renovator's Old Mill
Millers Falls
MA 10349
General supplies.

T.J. Ronan Paint Corp.
749 East 135th Street
Bronx NY 10454
Manufacturers of Japan colors.

Arthur Sanderson & Sons
979 Third Avenue
Suite 103
New York NY 10022
Hand-printed wallpapers.

Sappnos Paint
801 West Diversey
Chicago IL 60614
Suppliers of specialist brushes.

Sepp Leaf Products, Inc.
381 Park Avenue South
New York
NY 10018
Suppliers of gilding materials.

Stencil House of New Hampshire
PO Box 109
Hooksett
New Hampshire 03106
Stencils, acrylic paints, stencil adhesive, brushes, brush cleaners. Mail order only.

Stencil World
1456 Second Avenue
Box 175B
New York NY 10021
Decorative stencils and supplies. Mail order only.

The Stulb Company
PO Box 597
Allenstown
Pennsylvania 18105
Manufacturers of Williamburg buttermilk paint colors.

Leo Uhlfelder Company
420 South Fulton
Avenue
Mount Vernon NY
10553
Importer and manufacturer of gold leaf and brushes.

Utrecht Manufacturing Corp.
33-35th Street
Brooklyn NY 11232
General art supplies.

Western Sign Supply
4701 Coliseum Way
Oakland CA 94601
Suppliers of gilding materials.

Sherwin Williams
101 Prospect Avenue
Cleveland OH 44115

Winsor & Newton, Inc.
11 Constitution Avenue
Piscataway NJ 08855
Artists' paints and brushes.

S. Wolf and Sons
771 Ninth Avenue
New York NY 10019
Suppliers of paints and specialist brushes.

Wood Finishing Supply Company, Inc.
100 Throop Street
Palmyra NY 14522
Mail order glazes, Japan colors, steel combs, pinstriping tools, gold leaf, brushes and varnishes.

Woodcraft Supply Corp.
41 Atlantic Avenue
Woburn MA 01888

Woodcrafters Lumber Sales, Inc.
212 Northeast Sixth
Avenue
Portland OR 97232
Paint strippers, varnishes, brushes, speciality moldings and architectural elements.

Woodcrafter's Supply Corp.
5331 Sinclair Road
Columbus OH 43229
Paint strippers and varnishes.

Woodworker's Store
21801 Industrial
Boulevard
Rogers
MN 55374
Paint strippers, brushes, varnishes and wood fillers.

MUSEUMS

American Museum
Claverton Manor
Bath BA2 7BD
England

Chateau de Compiegne
60205 Compiegne
France

Kenwood House
Hampstead Lane
London NW3 7JR
England

Knole
Sevenoaks
Kent TN15 0RP
England

The Morris-Jumel Mansion
1765 Jumel Terrace
New York NY 10032
USA

Nostell Priory
Doncaster Road
Nostell
Nr. Wakefield
West Yorkshire
WF4 1QE
England

Palais de Versailles
Versailles
Nr. Paris
France

Palazzo Ducale
Piazza Sordello
Mantua
Italy

Plas Newydd
Llanfairpwll
Anglesey
Gywnedd
LL61 6EQ
Wales

Sir John Soane Museum
13 Lincolns Inn Fields
London
WC2A 3BP
England

St Fagan's Folk Art Museum
St Fagan's
Cardiff
CS5 6XB
Wales

The Vyne
Sherburne St John
Basingstoke
Hampshire
RG26 5DX
England

Index

Index

Left:
**Wooden panelling in an 18th century
townhouse is painted in several shades to
accentuate the three-dimensionality of the
mouldings.**

Acknowledgments

The authors and publishers would like to thank the following house-owners, interior designers, antique dealers, museums and stately homes for allowing special photography:

Jane and Alastair Brown
Mike Chalon
chateau de Compiegne
chateau d'O
Liz and Jim Cherry
Comoglio
Colleen Covington
Dan Cruikshank
Dick Dumas
Hannerle Dehn
Clifford Ellison
Piers Feetham
Steven and Sandra Gibbons
Christophe Gollut
Vera Gordon
Richard Gray
Linda Gumb
Mills van Gyk
Maria Luisa Condesa Vda de Foxia
Jenny Hall
Tony Heaton
Tom Hickman
Jonathan Hudson

Julian Humphreys
Richard Hampton Jenrette
Kenwood House
Stephen Mack
Trevor Micklem
Giumond Mounter
Morris Jumel Mansion
Lars Olssen
Lars Sjoberg
Jancis Page
Parham House
Jaime Parlade
Tom Parr
Buddy Rau
St Mary's, Bramber
Peter and Silvie Schofield
Giuseppi and Sarah Sesti
Sally Spillane and Robertson Leech
Skansen open-air museum in Stockholm
Dennis Severs
Temple Newson
Louis de Wet
Mary Wondrausch

The publishers would also like to thank the following individuals and companies for supplying materials for photography: Crown; Antoinette Putnam; Leslie Stubbs; and Benjamin John for demonstrating gilding.

Sources for props shown in the paint finish demonstrations:
The terracotta urn and trough were obtained from a garden store, the pine box from Ikea and the candlestick from Nice Irma's, Goodge St, London W1.
The pillar was constructed from plastic drainpiping by the paint artist. If you do not want to make your own, plaster pillars can be obtained from mouldings suppliers.